NEW MERMAIDS

NEW MERMAIDS

General editor: Brian Gibbons
Professor of English Literature, University of Münster

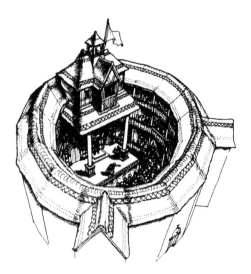

Reconstruction of an Elizabethan theatre
by C. Walter Hodges

NEW MERMAIDS

Ben Jonson

Every Man In His Humour

edited by Robert N. Watson

Professor of English
University of California, Los Angeles

A & C Black • London
WW Norton • New York

Second edition 1998
A & C Black (Publishers) Limited
35 Bedford Row, London WC1R 4JH

© *1998 A & C Black (Publishers) Limited*

First New Mermaid edition 1966
edited by Martin Seymour-Smith
first published by Ernest Benn Limited

© *1966, 1979 Ernest Benn Limited*

Published in the United States of America by
W. W. Norton & Company Inc.
500 Fifth Avenue, New York, N.Y. 10110

CIP catalogue records for this book
are available from the British Library
and the Library of Congress.

ISBN 13: 978-0-7136-4397-8

CONTENTS

ACKNOWLEDGEMENTS

I am deeply indebted to the previous editors of this play, including H. H. Carter, J. W. Lever, Martin Seymour-Smith, and Gabriele Bernhard Jackson, as well as to the great edition of Jonson's complete works by C. H. Herford and Percy and Evelyn Simpson. I have received superb research assistance from William Phelan, wise advice from A. R. Braunmuller and Brian Gibbons, and generous research funding from the Faculty Senate at UCLA and the William R. Kenan, Jr., Chair at Middlebury College.

INTRODUCTION

The Author

Ben Jonson was an astonishing character: a passionate figure with no apparent interest in love, a working-class child who became the exemplar of high court culture, a decorous classicist given to extreme drunkenness and murderous violence, a dedicated social climber who stubbornly sabotaged his own advancement, a moralistic writer who always seems to side with his rogues, a genius of comic drama who repeatedly withdrew bitterly from the theatre. Indeed, Jonson is a victim of his own success: having systematically used the mantles of classical literature and royal employment to conceal his common origins and wild tendencies, Jonson has convinced potential modern readers that he is boring, yet another formal snob in the literary establishment.

Jonson's father, a minister, died before his son was born in 1572; his stepfather was a bricklayer. Jonson's intelligence won him a scholarship to the prestigious Westminster School in London as a day-boy. There he met his lifelong mentor, William Camden, to whom *Every Man In His Humour* is dedicated. After apprenticing to his stepfather's trade, Jonson volunteered for the wars in Flanders, where – evidently not deeming that slow campaign dangerous enough – he reportedly challenged an enemy soldier to single combat, and killed him.

In his early twenties he married and had several children; the deaths of his first daughter and first son are lamented in his *Epigrams*. By 1597 he was acting and writing in the nascent theatre industry – and heading for jail. He had played the lead in Thomas Kyd's *Spanish Tragedy*, and was designated one of England's best tragic playwrights in Francis Meres's *Palladis Tamia* (1598) (though neither Jonson nor anyone else preserved any of the plays on which that judgement must have been based). But in August of 1597 he went to prison for his part in finishing a satiric play called *The Isle of Dogs* (also now lost). The next year, within a few days of the opening performance of *Every Man In His Humour*, Jonson killed fellow-actor Gabriel Spencer (who had been in prison with him) in a duel; he escaped execution – any man able to read Latin could claim exemption as a clergyman – but had his thumb branded and his belongings confiscated. To make things worse, he announced his conversion to Catholicism, a religion which was then illegal. After his release, he engaged in a prolonged literary brawl – now hyperbolically known as the War of the Theatres – with Thomas Dekker and

John Marston; he also boasted that he had battered Marston physically and taken his pistol.[1]

Despite disgrace and debt – or perhaps because of them – Jonson used his literary skills and scholarly reputation to gain the patronage of powerful aristocrats, whom he followed to their country houses – leaving his family back in London, to be devastated by the bubonic plague. He wrote fulsome elegies of praise to anyone who supported him, and wonderfully nasty epigrams against anyone who crossed him. When verse satires were made illegal, he invented the 'comical satire' mode of drama. *Sejanus* – like the later *Catiline*, a scholarly dramatization of the crises of ancient Rome – was hissed off the public stage, and earned him accusations of treason and Popery from a powerful courtier. After the Scottish King James succeeded Queen Elizabeth in 1603 and began selling knighthoods, Jonson co-authored a play called *Eastward Ho* that satirized Scots selling knighthoods, landing him again in prison in 1605.

Jonson soon re-emerged to write a series of great and popular comedies – first *Volpone*, then *Epicoene*, *The Alchemist*, and *Bartholomew Fair* – as well as a number of his great lyric poems. During these same years, having worked his way back into favour (partly by helping the government track down his fellow Catholics in the aftermath of the Gunpowder Plot), he became James's leading author of masques: elaborately produced ceremonial allegories designed to instruct and flatter the high-ranking persons who watched and often performed them. But he feuded bitterly with the physical architect of these productions, Inigo Jones, and the new King, Charles I (1625–49), turned to other authors. Jonson was even hired by Sir Walter Ralegh to tutor Ralegh's son in Paris – until the drunken Jonson (close to three hundred pounds weight of him by this time) was carted mockingly through the streets by his tutee. Virtually every claim to glory brought with it a threat of disgrace: along with the instances already mentioned, the early *Poetaster*, the mid-career *Epicoene*, and the late *Devil is an Ass*, each somehow landed him in trouble with the authorities.

Jonson's lifelong struggle to construct and project a dignified self through his literary art culminated in the 1616 Folio of his *Works*. Despite some mockery of the idea of presenting mere 'plays' under the grand traditional title of 'Works', Jonson had become a revered figure, a kind of poet laureate, winning honorary degrees, state employment, and a pension (including an annual barrel of wine). The 'Tribe of Ben', a loose association of leading Cavalier poets, worshipped him as their 'father' at many bibulous occasions. Still, disasters befell him, including a fire that destroyed his books and papers in 1623, and a stroke in 1628 that left him palsied – and a far less successful comic playwright – until his death in 1637.

---

[1] *Conversations with Drummond*, lines 284–6, in H&S, I, 140.

A Summary of the Plot

A letter from the young gallant Wellbred to his friend Edward
Knowell, accidentally delivered to Edward's father instead, con-
firms Old Knowell's fear that his son has fallen in with disrespectful wastrels who enjoy sex and poetry. So he sets off for the Old
Jewry to spy on his son's rendezvous, while the wily family servant
Brainworm plots to foil him. Edward brings along his foolish
country cousin Stephen, enamoured with the idea of himself as a
gentleman, to compare with Wellbred's foolish urban companion
Matthew, enamoured with the idea of himself as a melancholy
lover. In the lowly house of the water-carrier Cob and his wife Tib,
Matthew visits the cowardly braggart soldier Bobadill, who teaches
him supposedly infallible sword-fighting techniques to use against
the blunt, irascible Downright.

Wellbred lives nearby with his brother-in-law, the jealous merchant Kitely. Late for business meetings, but afraid to leave his wife
unguarded, Kitely vacillates miserably before indirectly admitting
his fears to his servant Cash. Edward arrives to hear Bobadill
inventing grandiose war-stories, while Stephen imitates Bobadill's
exotic oaths. Bobadill beats Cob for condemning the use of
tobacco, and the merry Justice Clement who hears Cob's complaint
almost jails him for the same reason.

Meanwhile, disguised as a beggared war-veteran, Brainworm
sells a worthless rapier to Stephen, and himself to Old Knowell as
an assistant, misinforming him that Edward has gone to Cob's
house. In a new disguise, as Justice Clement's assistant, Brainworm
then sends Kitely away again so that Edward can marry Kitely's
sister, Bridget, whom Matthew has been courting ineffectually.
Soon Kitely, his wife, Old Knowell, and Cob all come pounding on
the door of Cob's house, each assuming it has become a brothel
with Tib as its mistress and the others as its customers.

Downright at last gets hold of Bobadill and thrashes him, while
Stephen makes off with Downright's cloak, leading each of them to
be arrested (by Brainworm, in yet another disguise), and brought to
Justice Clement. Clement finally sorts out the entire truth, praising
Brainworm's cleverness, endorsing Edward's marriage and literary
interests, defending Tib's reputation, burning Matthew's plagiar-
ized poems, and banishing him and the discredited Bobadill from
the closing wedding-feast.

Sources and Descendants

Every Man In His Humour is fundamentally without sources,
except for the actual street-scenes of Elizabethan London, which
Jonson here replicates with a vivid specificity that recalls Dutch

painters of the same era. Jonson's supposed inspiration in the mode of 'humours' drama – George Chapman's commercially successful *An Humourous Day's Mirth* (1597) – provides only the idea of a decentralized plot in which a clever man justifiably tricks some foolish aristocrats. More relevant is the classical mode known as New Comedy, in which a wily servant helps a young man, suspected of wastrel behaviour, to marry against his vigilant father's wishes. New Comedy certainly provides the skeleton of Jonson's plot, which he dresses in the peculiar fashions and delicate proprieties of his own society.

But Jonson's heart is, characteristically, not in the love story; and neither of the play's most vivid characters have anything to do with it. The boastful coward Bobadill may derive from the classical *miles gloriosus*, perhaps even from Shakespeare's Falstaff, and the jealous miser Kitely may derive from the *Pantalone* of Italian Renaissance *commedia dell'arte*. Both have appeared in thousands of forms in every genre of comic writing, however, and Jonson's portraits of them have touches that are purely his own.

If *Every Man In* lacks roots, it is nonetheless rich in branches. Much of the genre called city comedy springs directly from this play; and in this and later plays, Jonson invents both the form and substance of most Restoration comedy, a world of fools and fops and jealous husbands where idle but urbane young gallants, in the process of capturing the most desirable women, wittily expose and exploit various social affectations. In a broader sense, Jonson – paradoxically, by concentrating specifically on Jacobean London – anticipates the centrifugal plotting and the metatheatrical irony of modern absurdist and existential dramatists such as Pinter, Beckett, Sartre, and Pirandello. The jokes may at first seem to be on the foolish characters, then on those who obey or applaud dramatic conventions, but they are finally on all of us who unconsciously equate the universe with a story in which we play the hero. By creating a play that explores the chaos and theatricality of human existence – the ways in which life, deprived of meaningful narrative shape, chooses to imitate art – Jonson creates philosophical insight and artistic revolution under the guise of localized realistic observation. The apparent contradiction is a false one: for Jonson (as for Freud), truth is found in laughter, and both (not the devil) are found in the details.

The Play

Virtually every time *Every Man In His Humour* has been revived, from early in the seventeenth century to late in the twentieth, commentators have professed amazement that a play relying less on plot and love than on the fashionable slang and eccentric manners of a bygone age could survive.[2] But it has. Ben Jonson's drama is a time-machine: just as his tragedies brought classical Rome into *verbatim* presence for Jacobean Londoners, his comedies bring Jacobean London into presence for us. Nowhere is this more true than in the Folio version of *Every Man In His Humour*: as the play begins we find that we have awakened in a very distant but very ordinary world, with new but oddly familiar companions. An old man stretches in the morning sunshine and worries about his son, who he hopes is doing schoolwork but he fears is sleeping off some combination of sex and alcohol. A careless postman delivers an invitation to the father instead of the son, and the plot is off and running until suppertime. A businessman lines up his day's appointments while fretting about his marriage. A water-carrier gets ready to begin the first deliveries of the day, while in a sordid room upstairs a braggart steadies himself to prop up his image for one more day, asking his landlady to get rid of the piss (or perhaps vomit) from the previous night's beer and to provide the first beer of the morning.[3]

Every Man In is innovative comedy precisely because it is business as usual. The roadside negotiations between Stephen and Brainworm over the sword may be outdated in their commodity and coinage, but not at all in their character: the hustling salesman passes off his inferior product as the fancy imported kind, flattering the buyer's judgement and asking him merely to offer a fair price, while the buyer, after hollowly demanding the salesman's lowest price, ends up buying the product more for pride and self-image than for any real need. Jonson's London may have been, as many scholars claim, a society rapidly and radically shifting from an archaic feudal system toward modern capitalism, but this transaction is as old as Plautus, and as recent as your last shopping trip.

So while Jonson may – proudly – deny us the romantic transcendences of Shakespearean comedy, he does offer a revelation of

---

[2] An anonymous reviewer of Garrick's production for the *London Chronicle* in 1757 calls it 'a Proof of an uncommon Genius to entertain us at the Time of Day with Ideas and Manners totally obliterated. It shews that the Painter's Pencil must have been faithful to Nature, otherwise we should hardly please ourselves, at present, with Portraits whose Originals are no more.' In his 1783 *Dramatic Miscellanies*, Thomas Davies comments that 'Of all our old playwrights, Jonson was the most apt to allude to local customs and temporary follies. ... It was a constant complaint of the old actors, who lived in Queen Anne's time, that if Jonson's plays were intermitted for a few years, they could not know how to personate his characters....' Quoted in R. V. Holdsworth, ed., *Every Man in His Humour and The Alchemist: A Casebook* (London: Macmillan, 1978), p. 64 and p. 46.

[3] Anne Barton, *Ben Jonson, dramatist* (Cambridge: Cambridge Univ. Press, 1984), p. 46, describes, with characteristic lucidity, this evocation of daily urban life.

transhistorical human tendencies, as they manifested themselves at a specific historical moment, which encouraged role-playing in the cause of social-climbing.[4] The ridiculous characters – the huffy, graceless Stephen, the mawkish plagiarist Matthew, the timid bully Bobadill – seem at least as lifelike as the supposedly normal, healthy characters. Jonson always claims to be a moral artist, but his gestures toward the ideal are half-hearted. He may not especially admire human beings, but he certainly seems to enjoy them; and his definition of the ethical centre is never as satisfying as his depiction of the outlying cases. The play could hardly be called realistic, but it is nonetheless the comedy of the real.

Even before the play begins, Jonson tells us what to watch for. The Prologue asks an audience trained to accept the hackneyed conventions and cheap effects of Elizabethan drama to appreciate a new, naturalistic mode of comedy instead:

> He rather prays you will be pleased to see
> One such, today, as other plays should be.
> Where neither Chorus wafts you o'er the seas;
> Nor creaking throne comes down, the boys to please;
> Nor nimble squib is seen, to make afeard
> The gentlewomen; nor rolled bullet heard
> To say, it thunders; nor tempestuous drum
> Rumbles, to tell you when the storm doth come;
> But deeds, and language, such as men do use;
> And persons, such as Comedy would choose,
> When she would show an image of the times,
> And sport with human follies, not with crimes ...
>
> (Prologue ll. 13–24)

This new mode promises to reform not only the social mores of London, by exposing its fakes and its fools, but also the literary manners of the time, by juxtaposing the fatuous and bombastic traditions of writers such as Shakespeare with Jonson's own satiric insight. As the wits seize control of the plot from the liars and their gulls, city comedy displaces the prodigal-son stories, vengeful duels, cuckolding farces, and erotic tragedies that had previously occupied the London stage, and that implicitly occupy the self-dramatizing, self-aggrandizing fantasies of the liars and gulls themselves.

Every man may be in his own humour, but they are all in Jonson's play, and therefore in his power. Life may imitate art, but not without paying some royalties. At moments Stephen, Matthew

---

[4] Stephen Greenblatt's deservedly influential *Renaissance Self-Fashioning* (Chicago: Univ. of Chicago Press, 1980) has shown how strong this encouragement was in Elizabethan London.

and Bobadill seem almost to believe their own lies: that they are truly a gentleman, a poet, a soldier. Old Knowell and Kitely seem eager to believe their own lurid fantasies, however humiliating: that a son or a wife has gone sexually astray. Old Knowell imagines himself the hero of a standard prodigal-son story, derived from Plautus and Terence, and commonplace in Elizabethan literature; so he sets out to rescue a son who needs no rescue. Kitely imagines himself the butt of a formulaic cuckolding plot; so he sets out to guard a wife who needs no guarding. By force of genre and readerly habit, we are likely to be taken along for the ride, and the fall.

Editors of Jonson's 'humours' plays feel obliged to explicate the Renaissance medical taxonomy that associated character traits with an imbalance among bodily fluids (one producing anger, another melancholy, and so on). But Jonson's use of the term is unorthodox. Distinguished early critics of the play such as William Congreve set the tone by defining a humour as a man's unique and unchangeable self, yet closer study suggests that it is virtually the opposite: a conventional fictional disguise the self chooses, which is by no means his own, and often the opposite of his true nature. Though the play bears some structural analogies to a humoural cure, Jonson's characters are driven less by chemistry than by fantasy; they are less what they eat than what they read. After all, Bobadill only pretends to be belligerent, and Matthew only pretends to be a melancholic lover. The idea that Jonson conceives the humours which control human action as essentially verbal rather than physical – not the fluids of one's body but the language of one's fluency – fits nicely with the evidence that he conceived the theatre and even the soul as more verbal than physical. His suggestion that 'Painting and carpentry are the soul of masque' in the 'Expostulation with Inigo Jones' is bitterly sarcastic. Language is power: because he can talk like a soldier and like a lawyer, Brainworm easily takes Old Knowell's secrets, Formal's clothing, Downright's and Stephen's money, finally even Downright's and Stephen's bodies into custody.

So if these victims seem like stock characters, it may be because they are 'humouring' themselves, selling to themselves or to the world a formulaic idea of their natures and their status, mediated by words. All Stephen's efforts – practising 'the hawking and hunting languages', for example – are directed towards being called a 'gentleman'. Bobadill's swordsmanship is all talk (plus a little mathematics), and when Stephen wants to become Bobadill, he simply emulates his oaths. When Matthew wants to prove himself romantically melancholy, he plagiarizes love-poetry. Even Cob tries to pun his way into a royal lineage. Kitely admits to having learned his final speech 'out of a jealous man's part in a play'. This pattern, greatly magnified in the revision of the play, allows Jonson to attack his literary rivals (a favourite occupation) because many of the characters are trying to play conventional dramatic roles of the period, which Jonson subjugates to the 'realities' of his own London scenes.

The most persistent form of joke in the play involves reinterpreting a word, usually to deflate it, as pretences are generally deflated in comedy. In the second scene of the play, for example, when Stephen asks Brainworm to 'truss me' for combat because the servant 'does so vex me', Brainworm answers, 'You'll be worse vexed, when you are trussed', 'trussed' by now meaning tied up like the victim bird he is. Before the scene is over, Stephen will find his words 'protest' and 'turn' turned against him similarly by Edward, and later in the play, when Stephen takes Downright's cloak intending to claim he 'bought it', Edward warns him, 'Take heed you buy it not too dear', meaning at the price of a beating. 'Used', 'boot', 'tried', 'bound', 'contents', 'host', 'shifts', even *incipere* undergo this kind of transformation. The micro level of language, where the wits expose the empty pretences of the fools' diction, resonates the macro level of character – Stephen's claim to be a gentleman, Bobadill's to be a soldier, Matthew's to be a melancholic Petrarch, even Kitely's to be a proud husband. Comedy loves the bursting of bubbles, and the pun is often the pin. The collapse of the word we intend into the word others hear neatly exemplifies the anxiety of a performative social existence.

By giving his fools such a theatrical approach to their own lives, Jonson is able to poke some meaningful fun at other playwrights as well. The plots of Jonsonian comedy are so bewilderingly complex because they reflect the process by which they were made: the author gathered up the full range of conventional story-lines and then subordinated them to a more urbane and realistic plot engineered by his own witty onstage alter ego. Whereas most comedy depends on formulas, Jonson's depends on the collapse of formulas.

In this sense, as I have argued elsewhere, the comedies are acts of theatrical imperialism.[5] Dryden wrote in *An Essay of Dramatick Poesie* that Jonson 'invades Authours like a Monarch; and what would be theft in other Poets is only victory in him'. Conventional plot-motifs and generic signatures appear within these plays in order to fail, to mislead both the naïve characters and a naïve audience. Celia and Bonario, for example, humiliatingly mistake *Volpone* for a sentimental melodrama, as Overdo mistakes *Bartholomew Fair* for a disguised-magistrate plot. The cheaters in *The Alchemist* control their victims by casting Drugger in a citizen comedy, Dapper in a fairy tale, Kastril in a roaring-boy story, Dame Pliant in a dynastic-marriage script, and the Puritans and Sir Epicure in their respective melodramas of God and Mammon.

---

[5] Robert N. Watson, *Ben Jonson's Parodic Strategy: Literary Imperialism in the Comedies* (Cambridge: Harvard Univ. Press, 1987).

Jonson observes in his *Discoveries* that

> our whole life is like a Play: Wherein every man, forgetfull of him-
> selfe, is in travaile with expression of another. Nay, wee so insist in
> imitating others, as wee cannot (when it is necessary) returne to our
> selves: Like children, that imitate the vices of Stammerers so long,
> that they become such.   (H&S, VIII, 597)

By recognizing this susceptibility – again, understood as a function
of language – characters such as Brainworm and Clement can
exploit and humiliate those who do not recognize it. By the same
process, Jonson can move the aforementioned War of the Theatres
onto a field where he is in complete command, carving out habit-
able territory for a genre – satiric city comedy – that suits his genius;
and, as his biography demonstrates, he is never shy about spilling
the blood of those who stand in his way. But he does encourage us,
with the traditional combination of carrot and stick, to become his
allies. If we appreciate this tactic we gain the pleasures of laughing
at the gulls who cannot let go of the old stories. If we resist, we
become the object of that scornful laughter.

The opening scene of *Every Man In His Humour* may lead us to
assume that this will be yet another Renaissance prodigal-son story,
because it begins with Old Knowell at centre stage striking a pose
as the patient but concerned father. His noble soliloquies are
exactly the sort that normally signal such a story; the only problem
is that his son Edward doesn't happen to be a foolish prodigal at all,
and the play doesn't turn out to be very impressed with Old
Knowell's efforts to protect him. Several critics have complained
that the letter Old Knowell intercepts hardly justifies his fears about
his son's misconduct, but that may be exactly the point: the father
hallucinates evidence to fulfil his conventional theatrical fantasy.
He assumes that Edward must be something like Stephen, because
disrespectful young men idly awaiting inheritances had always been
the objects of cautionary tales about wastrel behaviour; Downright
similarly misreads his brother Wellbred, again with little evidence,
as an immoral spendthrift exploited by parasitic companions.
Neither moralist can imagine that his younger kin will actually be a
hero of the story, because Jonson was creating a new type of
comedy designed to please the disrespectful young men idly awaiting inheritances who would support his livelihood, and that of
Brainworms like him, through the next century.

Editors diligently point out all the unacknowledged literary bor-
rowings – from Juvenal's *Satires*, Kyd's *Spanish Tragedy*, Terence,
Plautus, Ovid, Horace, and so on – in Old Knowell's admonitory
orations. But they assume they have simply caught incorrigible old
Ben stealing material again, whereas Jonson may have intended us
to catch Old Knowell unthinkingly echoing various grand literary

precedents. That intention would explain why Jonson bothers to tell us (as Shakespeare does about the comparable and perhaps derivative figure of Polonius) that Old Knowell was an actor and avid reader of literature in his youth: it encourages us to attribute the allusiveness to the character rather than the author.

We learn the same sort of thing about Kitely, in his offhand confession that he learned his wise closing remarks at a theatre. Like Old Knowell, he keeps expecting his life to follow the outlines of the literary models planted in his memory. Specifically, Kitely seems to convince himself that *Every Man In His Humour* will be a cuckolding farce – a fabliau, or a *commedia dell'arte* sketch. Socially his wife's inferior, and unable to impregnate her – acquiring cash and adopting Cash are uneasy compensations – the merchant feels his manhood threatened by Wellbred's idle presence. So he struggles wildly to avoid the role of pantaloon. But what finally humiliates him is not any unprincipled behaviour of his wife, but the principled behaviour of his creator, who refuses to justify his fears, or to make them anything more than a pathetic little subplot. Kitely ends up looking like a fool to us, not because his wife cuckolds him, but on the contrary, because he spends all his time trying to prevent something that none of the other characters seem to have the least intention of attempting. 'Horns i' the mind are worse than o' the head', Justice Clement finally tells him. When he hears that a young man has come to the house in his absence, Kitely says,

> Aye, I thought so: my mind gave me as much.
> I'll die but they have hid him i' the house,
> Somewhere; I'll go and search.   (IV.i.192–4)

If characters like Ford in Shakespeare's *Merry Wives of Windsor* are laughable because they can't find the men hidden in their wives' chambers, Kitely is laughable on a deeper psychological level because there isn't anyone for him to find.

Kitely agonizes over whether he dares to ask his servant Thomas to keep an eye on Dame Kitely while he's away. We may wonder why he is so afraid of asking, until we learn that Kitely's clearest dramatic ancestor, Hermino in Bentivoglio's *Il Geloso*, makes his fatal mistake by entrusting his wife to a servant who turns out to be a pimp. Since Thomas is just an ordinary loyal servant, Kitely again looks foolish for taking precautions against a threat that has more to do with literary conventions than with the reality of his world.

Jonson brings both Old Knowell's prodigal-son plot and Kitely's cuckolding plot to undignified and literally untimely ends. The false catastrophe comes in Act IV, Scene viii, when each of the deluded characters arrives at Cob's lowly house determined to conclude his own hackneyed story-line, only to encounter people playing out, with no less determination, no less hackneyed stories of their own.

Knowell believes he has found the brothel where his prodigal son does his prodigal things. Kitely and his wife are both convinced they have found the brothel where their spouse betrays them – confirmed by the fact that they find each other there. Cob himself thinks he's proved that his wife is a bawd. If this were a *commedia dell'arte* performance, they might all be right, because *commedia* characters are often caught misbehaving at a bawdy-house run by a low-comic couple. But *Every Man In* is a Jonson play, and characters who rely on conventional literary formulas make fools of themselves, not discoveries of others.

In the eighty-four lines of this scene, all hell breaks loose – and hell is other people. Old Knowell arrives at Cob's house and threatens to call the police if they fail to produce his son, who of course isn't there. Dame Kitely shows up, expecting to catch her husband with his paramour – though of course he doesn't have one. Seeing her, Old Knowell immediately decides that she must be the woman his son (who isn't fooling around) is fooling around with. Tib, the lady of the house, is so bewildered by Old Knowell's bizarre accusations that she locks the door, which Dame Kitely sees as further proof that her husband is carrying on somewhere inside. Kitely then arrives, expecting to trap Dame Kitely with her paramour, though she doesn't have one either.

Old Knowell now decides that Dame Kitely's accusations are 'but a device, to balk me withal', and when Kitely comes in, Knowell instantly deduces that Kitely must be his son in disguise. This is the work of what psychologists call cognitive dissonance: instead of surrendering their theatrical fantasies, these fools add further conventional plots to explain away any events discordant with the conventional plot they expected, like Renaissance astronomers positing epicycles to preserve an earth-centred view of the universe. Perhaps depicting such solipsistic folly provided Jonson with some distance from, some leverage on, his own massive egoism.

Kitely looks back at Old Knowell, and accuses him of being the old lecher who has seduced Dame Kitely, who concludes that this accusation is a trick of her husband's to cover up his own lecherous visit to this house, of which she assumes Tib is the bawd. Cob overhears that accusation, which he takes as confirmation of his long-standing fantasy of Tib's infidelity. All of these deluded characters congratulate themselves on their detective-work in pompous speeches of outraged virtue that owe more to literary formulas than to spontaneous feelings.

The truth is that young Edward and his wily servant Brainworm have arranged all these misunderstandings to divert everyone who might prevent Edward's marriage to Bridget, including Edward's father (Old Knowell) and Bridget's brother (Kitely), as well as her inferior suitor (Matthew). All the fantasies of the fools have been deliberately staged by this more witty group, clearing an offstage space for their triumphant performance of classical New Comedy. By the same trick, Jonson has cleared the same sort of generic space for himself.

All the other plots end by failing to end triumphantly at the moment their players are prepared to take their bows. How could they know, within the play-world, that they aren't yet in the fifth act? Cob's house is a theatre full of anti-climaxes. The common complaint about *Every Man In His Humour* – that its plot is confusingly fragmentary – overlooks Jonson's sweet new uses of diversity. Because he keeps the action within a single day and a small area (he was worshipped in the Neoclassical period for respecting the 'dramatic unities' as then understood), Jonson can afford to reflect the bewildering multiplicity of urban life, which more conventional plays must subordinate to unitary plots. Edward and Brainworm's plot continues on in the fifth act as the winner in a sort of literary demolition derby: the last plot still running wins, and the triumph will belong to the one that can induce collisions among its competitors while avoiding them itself. Jonson then brings in Justice Clement, as a representation of his ideal audience, to crown the winner.

Brainworm certainly seems to be a surrogate of Jonson, and when he removes his disguise to ask Clement's forgiveness, Brainworm mimics the standard behaviour of an epilogue. The fifth act is, in a sense, the epilogue to a plot that consisted of the defeat of all the conventions that collide at Cob's house. It defends the play as Brainworm defends his actions, pointing out that he has actually performed the truest function of comedy precisely by wrecking these vulgar versions of the genre: he has embarrassed fools, exposed hypocrites, and helped young lovers elude the old father who would prevent them from marrying. Like Brainworm, Jonson poses as a servant of the older generation's plots, but actually undermines those plots to enable the birth of a new generation of comedy.

Every Man In His Humour is not only one of Jonson's greatest successes, it is also arguably his most characteristic work, mixing imitation of ancient Greek and Roman literary motifs with mockery of his local contemporaries, and aggrandizing himself in the process. Contrary to post-Romantic assumptions, Jonson was best able to tell deep personal truths by close imitation of classical models (as in his epitaph 'On My First Son'), and here he shows the local realities of Jacobean London by mimicking the form of classical comedy. And (as in the love-lyric 'My Picture Left in Scotland') he insists on remaining visible in the foreground of his works, here by dividing himself prismatically into several of the most admirable characters. He associates himself not only with Brainworm, but also with Justice Clement, whose military experience allows him to judge soldiers (a claim Jonson makes for himself in *Poetaster*), and

whose behaviour as both an imperious official moralist and a forgiving theatrical madcap neatly embodies the contradiction in
Jonson's own attitude toward authority. Indeed, the play's reluc-
tance to challenge Clement's complacency, as even the best aristocratic characters are challenged, makes the Justice the least
appealing part of the play for many readers.

Jonson is visible in the 'rustical' Downright as well, a cudgel- and
(in the Folio) proverb-wielding critic of urban social follies who
shares the conflicts of Jonson's moralism, instinctively tending
toward violent indignation, but intellectually sensitive to decorum
and the obligation to yield to legal authorities. Like Macilente,
Volpone, Morose, Surly, Wasp, and Overdo in the great comedies
that follow, the choleric Downright is partly Jonson's effort to iso-
late his excessively satirical and judgemental tendencies in a character who must ultimately yield to more sociable principles. Jonson
could easily have been cast as Downright, since he was obviously a
physically intimidating figure.

Jonson is transparently present, finally, in Edward Knowell, the
young poet and romantic lead. Certainly the play would have con-
stituted a wish-fulfilment fantasy for the impoverished and power-
less Jonson of 1598: an unemployed young scholar wins the most
eligible woman and shows up the rich and powerful men of his city,
exposing their pretences, reforming their conduct, winning their
patronage, and increasing their respect for poetry.

As usual in Jonson's writing, the love-plot may be perfunctory,
and even Kitely's jealousy reflects an obsession more with control
than with sexuality:

> For opportunity hath balked 'em yet,
> And shall do still, while I have eyes and ears
> To attend the impositions of my heart.
> My presence shall be as an iron bar,
> 'Twixt the conspiring motions of desire:
> Yea, every look or glance mine eye ejects
> Shall check occasion, as one doth his slave,
> When he forgets the limits of prescription.   (II.i.194–201)

But Jonson's interest in gender is pervasive – and arguably perni-
cious, since it jeeringly affirms the stereotypical association between
effeminacy and homoerotic desire, allowing misogyny and homo-
phobia to affirm and amplify each other in the usual ways. Matthew,
Bobadill, and Stephen show marked interest in the beauty of their
own and each other's legs and hosiery; the fencing lesson is plausibly
an extended homoerotic farce; and Matthew's devotion to Bridget is
markedly formulaic and empty – indeed, a plagiarism (as his love-
poems are a plagiarism) of the more real and active heterosexuality
that Edward pursues into marriage. As elsewhere in Renaissance

drama – Shakespeare's *Twelfth Night* is an especially relevant example – such 'manly' assertiveness is contrasted with the immaturity implicitly underlying homosocial attachments and heterosexual timidity. While forgiving everyone else, Clement excludes Matthew and Bobadill from the final supper because they 'have so little of man in 'em' (V.i.202). It is again hard not to see Jonson himself in the brawling, hypermasculine Downright, who refuses to suffer fools or fops when he can instead make them suffer, and not hard to see phallic bravado in the way Downright's big cudgel dominates Stephen's droopy rapier, Matthew's mishandled one, and Bobadill's trembling one. The procreative hopes implicit in Edward's marriage contrast with the sterility of Kitely's family, which has grown only by the adoption of Cash – an archetypal fate for a miser.

Even the concern with cuckoldry has less to do with heterosexual desire (of which we see none in the play) than with homosocial competition (which motivates almost every pose and action). This emphasis, too, fits the author. Jonson's only recorded comment on his wife Ann called her 'a shrew yet honest', thus allowing himself a classic manly complaint while insisting that he had never been cuckolded, despite abandoning his wife's bed for five years; and he claimed that the only women who interested him sexually were other men's wives.[6] Onstage and off, Jonson's was a world of isolation and mediation, where even the most seemingly basic motives prove ulterior. The only realistic emotions occur in soliloquies, and even there the grounds are always delusional. Each fuelled by his own humour, each reading from a different second-hand script, the foolish characters can make contact only by bumping into one another. Communication always depends on go-betweens: Wellbred courts Bridget for Edward, Downright admonishes Wellbred for Kitely, Cash observes Dame Kitely for her husband (and Cash then has Cob observe for him), Formal speaks to Cob for Clement, and Brainworm – whose own business depends on keeping everyone else apart for a while – does just about everyone else's business, spying on Knowell for Edward while claiming to do the opposite, arresting Downright for Bobadill and Stephen for Downright in the role of someone he was hired to hire.[7] Whether we see this tireless and exhausting mediation as a reflection of Jonson's conflicts as a social being and a verbal artist, or as his critique of an already-decadent capitalist system (and money often seems to be a goal in itself in Jonson's comedies), it is the chaotic tendency that organizes this first great comedy, the sick joke at the hollow core of the first fruit of an absolutely unique genius.

[6] *Conversations with Drummond*, lines 254–5, 287–9, in H&S, I, 139–40.

[7] This pattern is brilliantly explicated by Jackson's introduction to the Yale edition of the play, p. 8.

The Play on the Stage

Every Man In His Humour began its stage life auspiciously, at the Curtain theatre late in 1598, with William Shakespeare listed first in the cast – perhaps meaning that he played Knowell, the first character to speak, and first in the *Dramatis Personae*, though it is tempting to suppose that he instead played Kitely, who was called Thorello in the early version of the play, and is strikingly echoed by Shakespeare's Othello a few years later. Also performing were Richard Burbage, who played the leads in Shakespeare's great tragedies; Will Slye and Will Kemp, Shakespeare's leading comedians; and John Heminges and Henry Condell, who would eventually produce the initial Folio edition of Shakespeare's works. The play was evidently a hit, performed 'Sundry times' according to the title-page of the Quarto, revived at Court in 1605 (the company was now the King's Men), and revived by them again in 1631.

Jonson's plays were extremely prominent after the Restoration. Killigrew's distinguished company performed *Every Man In* repeatedly at Drury Lane, and a contemporary observer said it was 'receiv'd with general Applause'.[8] But there was evidently no sustained interest, and when John Rich revived the play in 1725, he revised it as well, replacing seven of Jonson's characters with three of his own.

The great actor-producer David Garrick staged the play at Drury Lane in 1751 and for several years on tour thereafter, making some revisions (his complaints about outdated local references ring true for modern editors) and taking the role of Kitely, which he expanded for the occasion (at the expense of the 'groundling' comedy disdained in the period, such as most of Cob's role). Citing the extreme difficulty of Jonson generally and *Every Man In* particularly, Garrick claimed to have been preparing for this production for three years. Period costumes were used – a rarity at the time – and the event was sufficiently renowned for Sir Joshua Reynolds to paint a portrait of Garrick in the role. As Kitely, Garrick 'assumed an air of gaiety, but under that mask the corrosions of jealousy were seen in every feature ... the mixed emotions of his heart were strongly marked by his looks and the tone of his voice'.[9] Henry Woodward made Bobadill the role of his career, and acted it well over a hundred times; a 1794 eulogy delighted in 'Bobadill's fierce strut, or fiercer stare'.[10] The rival theatre at Covent Garden was obliged to stage a production of its own, even imitating the use

---

[8] R. G. Noyes, *Ben Jonson on the English Stage, 1660–1776* (Cambridge: Harvard Univ. Press, 1935), p. 250, quoting Langbaine's comment in 1691.

[9] Arthur Murphy, *The Life of David Garrick* (1801), I, 205–6; quoted by Noyes, p. 264.

[10] *The Thespian Magazine*, Sept. 1794, p. 347; quoted by Noyes, p. 285.

of period costumes. As a result, the play was acted every single year from 1751 to 1776, averaging six performances per season – a truly remarkable record for a seemingly dated and seemingly forgotten piece of drama.[11]

Though Jonson had drifted back into nearly total eclipse, the star actor and producer – this time Edmund Kean – again selected the role of Kitely when the play returned to Drury Lane in 1816 (William Macready would do the same at Covent Garden in the 1830s). Reviewing this production, the great critic William Hazlitt observed, as critics have ever since, how well Jonson comes alive on stage, despite the seemingly archaic portraits of Elizabethan mannerisms: 'This play acts much better than it reads ... Master Matthew, Master Stephen, Cob and Cob's Wife, were living in the sixteenth century. But from the very oddity of their appearance and behaviour, they have a very droll and picturesque effect when acted. It seems a revival of the dead ... Bobadill is undoubtedly the hero of the piece; his extravagant affectation carries the sympathy of the audience along with it'.[12]

Jonson, and indeed the entire genre of city comedy that had remained popular through the eighteenth century, 'all but disappeared from the stage' after the first quarter of the nineteenth.[13] But *Every Man In* provided a notable exception. In 1847 Charles Dickens arranged a private production, with himself in the role of Bobadill, which was so hugely popular that it moved (as a fundraiser for charities) into a public theatre, and then to a provincial tour. Herford and Simpson describe some of Dickens's stage business: 'at "This a Toledo? Pish" [III.i.149] he bent the sword into a curve; he leaned on his companion's shoulder when puffing out his tobacco smoke ... and he rattled off his arithmetic in Act IV, Scene [v], making an invisible sum of addition in the air, and scoring it underneath with an invisible line'.[14] One of the other actors in this 'success that outran the wildest expectations' reports that Dickens, though far from a polished performer, presented 'in Bobadill, after a richly coloured picture of bombastical extravagance and comic exaltation in the earlier scenes, a contrast in the later of tragical humility and abasement, that had a wonderful effect. But greatly as his acting contributed to the success of the night, this was nothing to the service he had rendered as manager.... He was the life and

[11] Noyes, p. 246. Carter traces performances continuing up through 1781.

[12] William Hazlitt, from *The Examiner*, 8 June 1816.

[13] Wendy Griswold, *Renaissance Revivals: City Comedy and Revenge Tragedy in the London Theatre, 1576–1980* (Chicago: Univ. of Chicago Press, 1986).

[14] H&S, IX, 184; based on C. and M. Cowden Clarke, *Recollections of Writers* (1878), pp. 310–11.

Charles Dickens as Bobadill, from a painting by C. R. Leslie,
RA, reproduced in *The Life of Charles Dickens*, ed. B. W.
Matz, vol. I (London: Chapman and Hall, 1911)

soul of the entire affair'.[15] Surely Dickens saw, in Jonson's comedy,
a brilliant ancestor of his own techniques of characterization:
Dickens's comic figures are nothing if not Jonsonian humours characters. Indeed, Jonson and Dickens stand out as the two great
chroniclers of the ordinary daily human comedy of London.

There have been three notable revivals of the play in
Shakespeare's own territory of Stratford-upon-Avon. The *Times*
review of F. R. Benson's 1903 production echoes Hazlitt's insight,
describing *Every Man In* as 'essentially an acting play ... which
needs the bustle and movement of the stage for its effect'.[16] But
Benson's Bobadill roused little enthusiasm, and the production was
an odd mixture of Elizabethan and modern characterizations.[17] In a

---

[15] H&S, IX, 182, from John Forster, *Life and Letters of Charles Dickens* (1872), II,
182–6.

[16] H&S, IX, 184.

[17] Ejner Jensen, *Ben Jonson's Comedies on the Modern Stage* (Ann Arbor: Univ. of
Michigan Research Press, 1985), p. 37.

livelier 1937 production, B. Iden Payne followed Garrick in trimming the archaic local references of the text, Godfrey Kenton made Kitely amusing despite many cuts in the references to cuckoldry, Donald Wolfit followed Woodward and Dickens in making Bobadill a comic centrepiece, and Knowell was made up to look like Shakespeare. In this case the *Times* acknowledged not just that staging distracted from the play's weaknesses, but that it elicited the play's hidden strengths: Payne's production 'brought out many diversions half hidden in the text'.[18] Most recently John Caird's straightforward and highly successful 1986 Royal Shakespeare Company production made good use of the Swan, a promontory stage designed to replicate the openness and intimacy of Jacobean theatres; again, Kitely (Henry Goodman) and Bobadill (Pete Postlethwaite) drew the warmest reviews.

Modern students of Shakespeare sometimes suspect that we evaluate his plays wrongly by focusing on readerly effects that could hardly have been perceived in the theatre (for which he was writing), only in the printed version (for which he evidently was not). With Jonson's comedies, with their intense and realistic sense of place, this favouring of page over stage is especially misguided, and actually works against the author. *Every Man In* needs to look like life. It shimmers with life's oscillations, back and forth: not just morning and evening, City and suburb, but the Bergsonian vacillations of Kitely between lingering home to guard his marriage and rushing off to run his business, the crossings of the stage that Brainworm can intercept in his various disguises, the professed quarrel-hunters Stephen and Bobadill fleeing again as the hunted. Only in the theatre, furthermore, could Jonson so convincingly demonstrate how theatrical modern urban life had become.

Note on the Text

This edition is based on facsimiles of Jonson's 1616 Folio, which he supervised carefully; I have preferred readings from what appear to be corrected stages of that printing. *Every Man In His Humour* is the first work in that historic volume. Jonson's earlier version of the play, performed in 1598 and published as a Quarto in 1601, had Italian names and settings, more direct uses of the name of God, harsher judgements of its characters, and a talkier final scene. Scholars disagree widely about the date of this revision, proposing anywhere from 1601 onward, with most guesses clustering around either 1605 or (especially for the Prologue) 1612, and recent biblio-

---

[18] Anonymous, *The Times*, 7 August 1937.

Edward Knowell (Simon Russell-Beale) lures Master Stephen
(Paul Greenwood) along on his journey to Old Jewry, as
Brainworm (David Haig) looks on, in I.ll of the Royal
Shakespeare Company production, 1986 (photo: Donald
Cooper © Photostage)

Bobadill (Pete Postlethwaite) uses Tib's bedstaffs to teach
Matthew (Philip Franks) his fencing techniques, in I.iv of the
RSC production, 1986 (photo: Donald Cooper © Photostage)

graphic studies suggesting that Jonson may still have been revising the play while other parts of the Folio were being printed. Scholars generally agree, however, about its high quality. I have used the Quarto only to clarify ambiguous points in the Folio text.

I have silently corrected small typographical errors that do not affect meaning, especially where authorized by corrections evident in the Second Folio (1640). The glossary notes record my attempts to repair the original typesetter's occasional carelessness about the distinction between prose and verse lines, and to replace Jonson's Continental practice of marking a new scene at each significant entrance with the modern practice that does so only when all characters have exited. At the beginning of each scene, the Folio lists all the characters who appear in that scene; I have replaced that group listing with individual entrances at the likeliest moment in the text. These and other added stage directions appear in square brackets. There are no truly substantive variants among surviving copies of the 1616 Folio; my few emendations are acknowledged in the glossary notes.

I have modernized spelling and punctuation, while trying to retain some impression of Jonson's characteristic verbal rhythms, which he conveyed by elisional apostrophes and heavy punctuation. A single sentence at IV.v.32–8 – by no means one of the play's longest – contains, in F, a semi-colon, an exclamation point, a colon, a question mark, a period, and thirteen commas. Even in punctuating his scripts, Jonson was a glutton, and a bully. But he had his reasons, some of them clarified by his *English Grammar*, others clarified by performance. Though I have generally retained Jonson's complex sentences, modern usage dictates reversing most of Jonson's colons and semi-colons, and eliminating excess commas where they do not seem to carry poetic or dramatic value. Thus, for example, where I.i.142–3 in F reads, 'This letter is directed to my sonne: / Yet, I am EDWARD KNO'WELL too', I have not only modernized the spelling of 'sonne', but also changed the colon to a semi-colon, because it marks a neutral pause between independent clauses, rather than the delivery of information to exemplify or prove what preceded the mark. I have left the comma after 'Yet' because, though few modern writers would include it, it creates no syntactical confusion, and may indicate a dramatically useful pause in the speaker's deliberation. I have eliminated the capitalization of the name as an archaic typographical effect, and the apostrophe as a persistent distraction that would not change a modern reader's pronunciation of 'Knowell' or illuminate any otherwise very obscure meaning. Conversely, where III.i.190–2 in F reads, 'I can compare him to nothing more happily, then a drumme; for euery one may play vpon him', I have not only reversed the old 'u' and 'v' typography and modernized to 'drum' and 'than', but also changed the semi-colon to a colon; and I have eliminated the commas as both essentially meaningless and incompatible with modern usage.

The following quotations (with accompanying grid co-ordinates) help to locate this insistently local play on the so-called 'Agas' map of London, created in the 1560s. The map (on the following pages) is adapted from *The A to Z of Elizabethan London*, ed. Adrian Prockter and Robert Taylor (London Topographical Society Publication no. 122, 1979, p. 10).

I.ii.81–83: Edward tells Stephen: 'I am sent for, this morning, by a friend i' the Old Jewry [E 13–17] to come to him. It's but crossing over to Moorgate [G 5]. Will you bear me company?'

I.iii.67–69: Cob reports that Matthew 'useth every day to a merchant's house, where I serve water, one Master Kitely's, i' the Old Jewry [E 13–17].'

II.ii.8–10: Brainworm says that 'my old master intends to follow my young, dry foot, over Moorfields [G–S 1–4] to London this morning.'

III.i.209: Brainworm tells Edward that Wellbred's letter 'blew you to the Windmill [F 13], and your father after you', and that (i. 216) Old Knowell is now 'At Justice Clement's house here in Coleman Street [D 6–F 12].'

III.ii.117–119: Kitely tells Cash, 'let one straight bring me word . . . To the Exchange [O 16–17] . . . Or here in Coleman Street, to Justice Clement's.'

III.iii.86: Cash reports that Kitely is 'At Justice Clement's . . . in the middle of Coleman Street [approx. E 9].'

IV.iv.2–3: Old Knowell reports encountering the disguised Brainworm 'begging o' the way, / This morning, as I came over Moorfields! [G–S 1–4].'

IV.iv.43–4: Brainworm directs Old Knowell to 'one Cob's House, a water-bearer that dwells by the wall [A 4–V 6].'

IV.iv.72–4: Formal invites Brainworm 'to the Windmill [F 13].'

V.i.158–9: Brainworm reveals the Edward and Bridget 'are ready to bespeak their wedding supper at the Windmill [F 13]' before being invited home to Justice Clement's [approx. E 9].

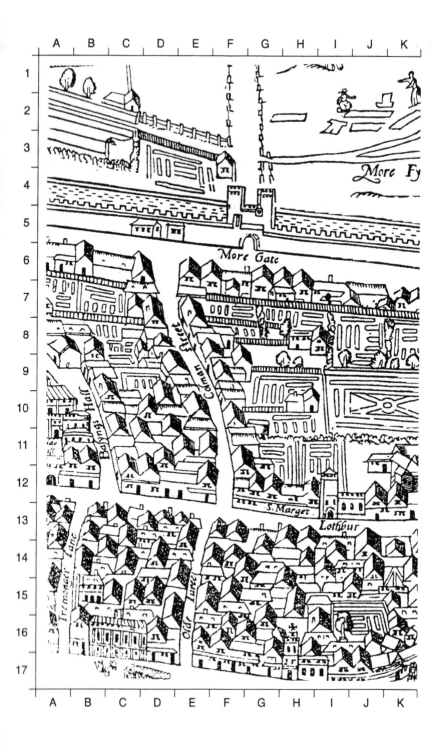

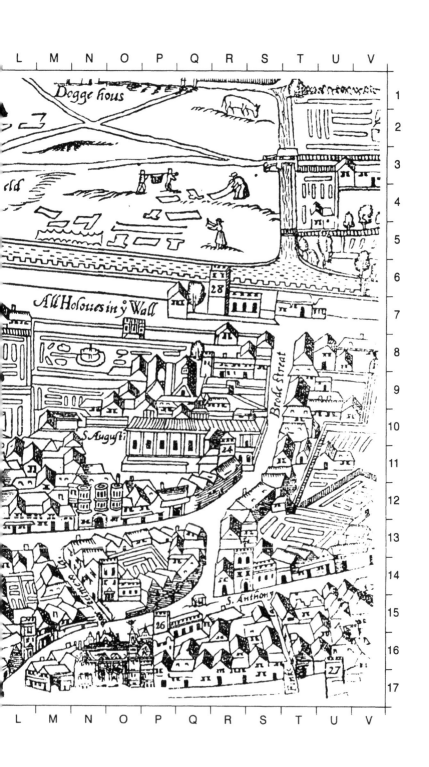

Dogge hous

All Holoues in y Wall

28

Brode Streat

S. Augusti

24

26

S. Anthony

27

ABBREVIATIONS

Carter	H. H. Carter, ed., *Every Man in his Humor* (New Haven: Yale Univ. Press, 1921)
Chalfant	Fran C. Chalfant, *Ben Jonson's London* (Athens: Univ. of Georgia Press, 1978)
Dent	R. W. Dent, *Proverbial Language in English Drama, Exclusive of Shakespeare, 1495–1616: An Index* (Berkeley and Los Angeles: Univ. of California Press, 1984)
Dent-S	R. W. Dent, *Shakespeare's Proverbial Language: An Index* (Berkeley and Los Angeles: Univ. of California Press, 1981)
F2	Ben Jonson, *Works*, Second Folio edition (London, 1640)
H&S	C. H. Herford, Percy Simpson, and Evelyn Simpson, eds., *Ben Jonson* (Oxford: Clarendon Press, 1925–52)
Jackson	Gabriele Bernhard Jackson, ed., *Every Man in his Humor* (New Haven: Yale Univ. Press, 1969)
Lever	J. W. Lever, ed., *Every Man in His Humour: A Parallel-text Edition of the 1601 Quarto and the 1616 Folio* (Lincoln: Univ. of Nebraska Press, 1971)
OED	J. A. Murray et al., eds., *A New English Dictionary* (Oxford: Oxford Univ. Press, 1888–1933)
Q	*Every Man in His Humour*, first Quarto edition (London, 1598)
Seymour-Smith	Martin Seymour-Smith, ed., *Every Man in His Humour* (London: Ernest Benn, 1966)
Tilley	M. P. Tilley, *A Dictionary of Proverbs in England in the Sixteenth and Seventeenth Centuries* (Ann Arbor: Univ. of Michigan Press, 1950); the proverbs can generally be traced under the same numbers in the indexes by R. W. Dent
Williams	Gordon Williams, *A Dictionary of Sexual Language and Imagery in Shakespearean and Stuart Literature*, 3 vols. (London: Athlone Press, 1994)

Citations of Shakespeare are based on *The Riverside Shakespeare*, ed. G. B. Evans (Boston: Houghton Mifflin, 1974)

FURTHER READING

Jonas Barish, *Ben Jonson and the Language of Prose Comedy* (Cambridge: Harvard Univ. Press, 1960); a pioneering analysis of the relationship between style and meaning

Anne Barton, *Ben Jonson, dramatist* (Cambridge: Cambridge Univ. Press, 1984); the most helpful and perceptive modern study of Jonson's plays

J. A. Bryant, 'Jonson's Revision of *Every Man in His Humor*', *Studies in Philology* 59 (1962), 641–50

A. Richard Dutton, 'The Significance of Jonson's Revision of *Every Man in His Humor*', *Modern Language Review* 69 (1974), 241–9

H. H. Carter, ed., *Every Man in His Humor* (New Haven: Yale Univ. Press, 1921); a scholarly parallel-text version of the play, with an informative introduction

Brian Gibbons, *Jacobean City Comedy*, 2nd ed., (London: Methuen, 1980); the best overview of play's genre, which Jonson developed into the mode that would attract the wittiest playwrights of subsequent decades

Jonathan Haynes, *The Social Relations of Jonson's Theater* (Cambridge: Cambridge Univ. Press, 1992); an historically alert study of the plays, with perceptive commentary on class issues in *Every Man In*

C. H. Herford, Percy Simpson, and Evelyn Simpson, *Ben Jonson* (Oxford: Clarendon Press, 1925–52); the great modern edition of the complete works, well annotated

R. V. Holdsworth, ed., *Every Man in His Humour and The Alchemist: A Casebook* (London: Macmillan, 1978); the only collection with multiple essays on this play, including some early criticism and stage reviews

Gabriele Bernhard Jackson, ed., *Every Man in his Humor* (New Haven: Yale Univ. Press, 1969); the most informative modern edition, with an excellent introduction

Alexander Leggatt, *Ben Jonson: His Vision and His Art* (London: Methuen, 1981); a perceptive overview of Jonson's writing, though it makes little mention of *Every Man In*

J. W. Lever, ed., *Every Man in His Humour: A Parallel-text Edition of the 1601 Quarto and the 1616 Folio* (Lincoln: Univ. of Nebraska Press, 1971); the best modern tool for studying the two versions of *Every Man In*

Lawrence Levin, 'Clement Justice in *Every Man in His Humour*', *Studies in English Literature* 12 (1972), 291–307

Russ McDonald, *Shakespeare and Jonson/Jonson and Shakespeare*

(Lincoln: Univ. of Nebraska Press, 1988); a vivid explication of the comparison that has controlled Jonson's modern reputation, with an extended comparison of *Every Man In* and *The Merry Wives of Windsor*

David R. Riggs, *Ben Jonson: A Life* (Cambridge: Harvard Univ. Press, 1989); a brilliant biography, rich in historical detail and psychoanalytic insight

Robert N. Watson, *Ben Jonson's Parodic Strategy: Literary Imperialism in the Comedies* (Cambridge: Harvard Univ. Press, 1987); provides a more extended application, to this play and others, of the argument outlined above

Robert N. Watson, ed., *Critical Essays on Ben Jonson* (New York: G. K. Hall, 1997); the most recent collection of Jonson criticism

Euery
MAN IN
HIS
HVMOVR.

A Comœdie.

Acted in the yeere 1598. By the then
Lord Chamberlaine his
Seruants.

The Author B. I.

IUVEN.

Haud tamen inuideas vati, quem pulpita pascunt.

LONDON,
Printed by WILLIAM STANSBY.

M. DC. XVI.

DEDICATION

TO THE MOST LEARNED, AND MY HONOURED FRIEND,
Master Camden, CLARENCEUX

SIR, There are, no doubt, a supercilious race in the world, who will esteem all office done you in this kind an injury, so solemn a vice it is with them to use the authority of their ignorance to the crying down of *poetry*, or the professors; but my gratitude must not leave to correct their error, since I am none of those that can suffer the benefits conferred upon my youth to perish with my age. It is a frail memory that remembers but present things; and, had the favour of the times so conspired with my disposition as it could have brought forth other, or better, you had had the same proportion and number of the fruits, the first. Now, I pray you to accept this: such, wherein neither the confession of my manners shall make you blush; nor of my studies, repent you to have been the instructor. And, for the profession of my thankfulness, I am sure it will, with good men, find either praise, or excuse.

Your true lover,
BEN. JONSON

DEDICATION This dedicatory letter is so elaborately mannered in syntax and diction that a modern paraphrase may serve better than many piecemeal glosses. The sense of the letter is: 'There are, no doubt, snobs who consider such dedications an insult, so seriously do they take themselves when their ignorance allows them loudly to condemn both poetry and those who practice it; but my gratitude must never cease to correct that error, since I am not the kind of person who will allow the benefits conferred on me in youth to be forgotten as I grow older. It is a weak memory that remembers only recent things; and if circumstances had been so suited to my disposition that I could have brought forth other or better works than this play, you would still have received as tribute the "first fruits" of my art. Now, I ask you to accept this: the kind of work that will not make you blush for what it shows about my manners, nor make you sorry you were my teacher for what it shows about my learning. And, because I have dedicated it to you in gratitude, I am sure the play will, from good men, receive either praise or forgiveness'.

Camden William Camden (1551–1623), a distinguished scholar, and Jonson's revered teacher at Westminster School, an excellent grammar school near Jonson's boyhood home

CLARENCEUX Camden's title (added to the Folio) as a high official in the Heralds' College, which researched the history and authorized the issuance of aristocratic titles

BRAINWORM In Renaissance English 'worm' could mean a whim or 'maggot' in the brain ... a streak of madness or insanity (OED *sb*. 11.b). So the name may suggest 'madcap'. 'Worm' may suggest the verbal and psychological bait he offers his victims, or perhaps the way he enters into the stereotypes and fantasies of those he manipulates.

the father's man Old Knowell's servant

gull a common Elizabethan term for a foolish, 'gullible' person

DOWNRIGHT plain and direct in speech or behaviour (sometimes implying bluntness of manner) (OED); perhaps a play on an old song called 'Downe right Squier'. A squire was a gentleman of near-aristocratic rank, often a country land-owner. Downright is stereotypically masculine, and – dominated by a choleric humour – quick to anger at the foppish dress, speech, and manners of the more effeminate men.

CLEMENT 'merciful', with a play on Clement's Inn, an Inn of Chancery (or preparatory law school) in London, where Shakespeare's Justice Shallow remembers being a 'mad' fellow in his youth (*2 Henry IV*, III.ii.14–15), as Clement is a 'mad, merry, old fellow' (III.iii.45).

COB a fish. Cf. Nashe, *Lenten Stuffe* (1599): 'Lord high regent of rashers of the coles and red herring cobs'; also a type of gull. A comic lower-class character, but often shrewd in mocking his social betters.

water-bearer a labourer who carried tankards from London's neighbourhood cisterns to private homes, which generally did not have their own water supplies

TIB a typical name for a woman of the lower classes ... Also ... a young woman of loose or low character, a strumpet (OED)

BOBADILL Editors have always associated this name with Boabdil, the Moorish king expelled from Spain. However, Cash's remark that he wishes Bobadill 'were at Santo Domingo' (III.iii.89–90) suggests the importance of Francisco de Bobadilla or Bovadilla, who succeeded Columbus as governor of Santo Domingo (the modern Dominican Republic) and, to culminate a series of ploys to win popularity with the Spaniards, sent Columbus back to Spain in chains. The character's name in Q is Bobadilla.

Paul's-man i.e. the type who loitered in the middle aisle of the earlier St. Paul's cathedral, a surprising favourite site for gossip and deal-making among London's rogues and gallants

THE PERSONS OF THE PLAY

KNOWELL an old gentleman
EDWARD KNOWELL his son
BRAINWORM the father's man
MASTER STEPHEN a country gull [Edward's cousin]
[GEORGE] DOWNRIGHT a plain squire
WELLBRED his half-brother [and Dame Kitely's brother]
JUSTICE CLEMENT an old merry magistrate
ROGER FORMAL his clerk
[THOMAS] KITELY a merchant
DAME KITELY his wife
MISTRESS BRIDGET his sister
MASTER MATTHEW the town gull
[THOMAS] CASH Kitely's man
[OLIVER] COB a water-bearer
TIB his wife
CAPTAIN BOBADILL a Paul's-man
[SERVANTS, etc.]

The Scene: London

5

3–4 *Yet ... age* i.e. the author of this play, however, has not been driven by poverty into feeding corrupt appetites of Jacobean audiences in order to keep his theatrical career going

7 *now* very recently

8 *weed* costume

10 *foot-and-half-foot words* elaborate diction (as notoriously practised by Jonson's bitter literary rival John Marston), with a jab at the unnatural metres such diction often imposes. The phrase appears as Jonson's translation of '*sesquipedalia verba*' in *De Arte Poetica*, by his greatest literary hero, Horace.

11 *York ... jars* The Wars of the Roses; here as elsewhere in *Every Man In*, the jab seems primarily directed at Shakespeare's history plays.

12 *tiring-house* dressing-room, the place where actors put on their theatrical attire, immediately behind the main stage at the Globe

16–18 *Nor creaking ... bullet* Jonson forswears not only the aforementioned tired and unrealistic plot devices, but also various cheap, commonplace special effects of the Renaissance theatre, such as a throne carrying a supernatural being down from the heavens (the classical *deus ex machina*), firecrackers to simulate lightning or diabolic powers, or rolled cannonballs to simulate thunder.

30 *monsters* something extraordinary or unnatural, or an animal deviating in one or more of its parts from the normal type (OED); again Jonson sets his professed naturalism against cruder forms of popular theatrical entertainment. Forms of this word appear repeatedly in the play.

PROLOGUE

Though need make many Poets, and some such
As art and nature have not bettered much;
Yet ours, for want, hath not so loved the stage,
As he dare serve th' ill customs of the age,
Or purchase your delight at such a rate,   5
As, for it, he himself must justly hate.
To make a child, now swaddled, to proceed
Man, and then shoot up, in one beard and weed,
Past threescore years; or, with three rusty swords,
And help of some few foot-and-half-foot words,   10
Fight over York and Lancaster's long jars;
And in the tiring-house bring wounds to scars.
He rather prays you will be pleased to see
One such, today, as other plays should be.
Where neither Chorus wafts you o'er the seas;   15
Nor creaking throne comes down, the boys to please;
Nor nimble squib is seen, to make afeared
The gentlewomen; nor rolled bullet heard
To say, it thunders; nor tempestuous drum
Rumbles, to tell you when the storm doth come;   20
But deeds, and language, such as men do use;
And persons, such as Comedy would choose,
When she would show an image of the times,
And sport with human follies, not with crimes –
Except, we make 'em such by loving still   25
Our popular errors, when we know they're ill.
I mean such errors, as you'll all confess
By laughing at them, they deserve no less;
Which when you heartily do, there's hope left, then,
You, that have so graced monsters, may like men.   30

A Note on Oaths

An oath is a 'solemn or formal appeal to God (or a deity or something held in reverence or regard) in witness of the truth of a statement' or a 'promise corroborated by such an appeal' (OED). The oaths Bobadill uses to impress the fools – 'By the foot of Pharaoh!' – begin with an implied 'I swear'. Other characters begin their oaths with an implied 'I swear by God', producing strange forms such as ''Slid', meaning '[I swear by God]'s [eye]lid'. These compressions serve partly to provide efficiencies or eccentricities of speech, but also partly to accommodate – and parody – censorship laws enacted in 1605/6 which forbade players to use the Lord's name in vain; the 1601 Quarto version of the play was far less delicate. Lines may begin with exclamations such as ''Heart', 'Mass' (i.e. 'I swear by the Mass') 'Marry' ('I swear by the Virgin Mary') and 'Faith' ('In faith'). Such forms are common in Renaissance English drama, as presumably they were in Renaissance London, and are explained here in order to avoid highly repetitive glossary notes in the text.

EVERY MAN IN HIS HUMOUR

Act I, Scene i

[*Enter*] KNOWELL, BRAINWORM

KNOWELL
A goodly day toward! And a fresh morning! Brainworm,
Call up your young master: bid him rise, sir.
Tell him I have some business to employ him.
BRAINWORM
I will sir, presently.
KNOWELL   But hear you, sirrah,
If he be at his book, disturb him not.
BRAINWORM   Well sir.   [*Exit*]   5
KNOWELL
How happy yet should I esteem myself
Could I (by any practice) wean the boy
From one vain course of study he affects.
He is a scholar, if a man may trust
The liberal voice of fame in her report,   10
Of good account in both our universities,
Either of which hath favoured him with graces;
But their indulgence must not spring in me
A fond opinion, that he cannot err.
Myself was once a student; and, indeed,   15
Fed with the self-same humour he is now,
Dreaming on nought but idle poetry,

---

1 *toward* beginning, imminent, promising
4 *presently* immediately
  sirrah a term of address used when speaking to men or boys, expressing ... authority on the part of the speaker (OED)
5 *at his book* studying
7 *practice* tactic
10 *liberal* free in bestowing; bountiful, generous, open-hearted (OED)
11–12 *both ... graces* Jonson himself held honorary degrees from Oxford and
  Cambridge.
14 *fond* foolish
15–20 *Myself ... knowledge* Adapted from a speech by Hieronimo – a famous role
  Jonson himself had played – at the beginning of the final Act of Kyd's *Spanish
  Tragedy*, perhaps to show that Old Knowell is still unwittingly in the hold of that
  early literary interest.

9

That fruitless and unprofitable art,
Good unto none, but least to the professors,
Which then I thought the mistress of all knowledge;   20
But since, time and the truth have waked my judgement,
And reason taught me better to distinguish
The vain from th' useful learnings.

[*Enter* STEPHEN]

Cousin Stephen!
What news with you, that you are here so early?
STEPHEN
Nothing, but e'en come to see how you do, uncle.   25
KNOWELL
That's kindly done, you are welcome, coz.
STEPHEN
Aye, I know that, sir, I would not ha' come else. How do
my cousin Edward, uncle?
KNOWELL
Oh, well, coz, go in and see; I doubt he be scarce stirring
yet.   30
STEPHEN
Uncle, afore I go in, can you tell me an' he have e'er a book
of the sciences of hawking, and hunting? I would fain
borrow it.
KNOWELL
Why, I hope you will not a-hawking now, will you?
STEPHEN
No, wusse; but I'll practice against next year, uncle: I have 35
bought me a hawk, and a hood, and bells, and all; I lack
nothing but a book to keep it by.

---

19 *professors* practitioners
20 *mistress* reigning authority
25 *e'en* only, precisely
26 *coz* short for cousin, a more general term of affinity than in modern usage
29–30 *I doubt ... yet* i.e. I suspect he's barely awake yet
31 *an' he have e'er a book* whether he has any books; here and throughout the play,
   'an'' means 'if'
32 *fain* gladly
35 *wusse* variant of iwis: certainly, assuredly (OED)
   against in preparation for
36 *a hood, and bells* A hood was placed over the head of a hawk to blind it when
   not pursuing game (OED); a small, shrill bell was attached to each leg of the
   hawk to help locate it in dense foliage.
37 *to keep it by* i.e. to tell me how to train and care for the hawk

KNOWELL

Oh, most ridiculous.

STEPHEN

Nay, look you now, you are angry, uncle; why you know,
an' a man have not skill in the hawking and hunting lan-   40
guages nowadays, I'll not give a rush for him. They are
more studied than the Greek or the Latin. He is for no gallant's company without 'em. And by gad's lid I scorn it, I,
so I do, to be a consort for every humdrum; hang 'em,
scroyles, there's nothing in 'em i' the world. What do you   45
talk on it? Because I dwell at Hogsden, I shall keep
company with none but the archers of Finsbury? Or the citizens that come a-ducking to Islington ponds? A fine jest, i'
faith! 'Slid, a gentleman mun show himself like a gentleman. Uncle, I pray you be not angry, I know what I have to   50
do, I trow, I am no novice.

KNOWELL

You are a prodigal absurd coxcomb; go to.
Nay, never look at me, it's I that speak.
Take't as you will sir, I'll not flatter you.
Ha' you not yet found means enow to waste   55
That which your friends have left you, but you must

---

41 *rush* a single-stalked weed, used as a type of something of no value or import-
     ance (OED); Stephen's phrase is proverbial (Tilley S917).

42 *He is for no* i.e. He does not qualify for any

43 *by gad's lid* The first of countless oaths in the play, sometimes difficult to recog-
     nize because censorship forbade more direct forms such as 'By God's eyelid'; fur-
     ther shortened to ''Slid' at l. 49 below. See the 'Note on Oaths' above.

44 *humdrum* a dull, monotonous, commonplace fellow (OED)

45 *scroyles* scoundrels, wretches (OED)
     nothing in 'em i' the world i.e. nothing worthwhile about them whatsoever

46 *Hogsden* Hoxton, a suburb north of London with fields popular at the time for
     recreation. Also for duelling: Hogsden is where Jonson killed his colleague
     Gabriel Spencer soon after they first performed this play.

47 *Finsbury* fields where this outdated art was practised, perhaps by those who –
     like Stephen – pretended to be aristocrats

48 *Islington ponds* a popular duck-hunting spot on the outskirts of Jacobean
     London, near Finsbury

49 *mun* must

51 *trow* trust, believe

52 *coxcomb* fool
     go to A common, vague, dismissive Renaissance colloquialism, something like
     the modern 'get lost', 'don't be ridiculous', or 'shame on you'.

53 *never look at me* i.e. don't give me that (shocked, indignant) look

55 *enow* enough

Go cast away your money on a kite,
And know not how to keep it, when you ha' done?
Oh it's comely! This will make you a gentleman!
Well, cousin, well! I see you are e'en past hope   60
Of all reclaim. Aye, so, now you are told on it,
You look another way.
STEPHEN   What would you ha' me do?
KNOWELL
What would I have you do? I'll tell you kinsman:
Learn to be wise, and practice how to thrive,
That would I have you do; and not to spend   65
Your coin on every bauble that you fancy,
Or every foolish brain that humours you.
I would not have you to invade each place,
Nor thrust yourself on all societies,
Till men's affections, or your own desert,   70
Should worthily invite you to your rank.
He that is so respectless in his courses
Oft sells his reputation at cheap market.
Nor would I, you should melt away yourself
In flashing bravery, lest while you affect   75
To make a blaze of gentry to the world,
A little puff of scorn extinguish it,
And you be left like an unsavoury snuff,
Whose property is only to offend.
I'd ha' you sober, and contain yourself: 80
Not, that your sail be bigger than your boat;

---

57 *kite* bird of prey considered inferior to the hawk: 'It is impossible to make a good
     hawk of a kite' (Tilley K114)

58 *ha' done* have purchased it

59 *comely* At least three meanings apply, sarcastically: attractive, appropriate,
     noble.

61 *on* of

66 *bauble* a showy trinket or ornament such as would please a child, a piece of
     finery of little worth (OED)

67 *brain that humours you* i.e. notion (or, possibly, con-man) that pleases your whim

70 *desert* deserving, merit

72 *respectless* heedless, reckless (OED); also, failing to show respect for self or
     others

74–6 *Nor would ... blaze of gentry* i.e. Nor do I wish you to expend your resources
     on gaudy clothes, for fear that while you are seeking to display your nobility....
     Knowell constructs an extended metaphor comparing Stephen to a candle (cf.
     Tilley C49: 'to go out like a candle in a snuff').

81 *your sail ... boat* Cf. the proverb 'make not your sail too big for your boat'
     (Tilley S24).

But moderate your expenses now (at first),
As you may keep the same proportion still;
Nor stand so much on your gentility,
Which is an airy and mere borrowed thing,   85
From dead men's dust and bones, and none of yours
Except you make or hold it. Who comes here?

[*Enter a* SERVANT]

SERVANT
Save you, gentlemen.
STEPHEN
Nay, we don't stand much on our gentility, friend; yet, you
are welcome, and I assure you, mine uncle here is a man of   90
a thousand a year, Middlesex land; he has but one son in
all the world, I am his next heir (at the common law),
Master Stephen, as simple as I stand here, if my cousin die
(as there's hope he will), I have a pretty living o' mine own
too, beside, hard by here.   95
SERVANT
In good time, sir.
STEPHEN
In good time, sir? Why, and in very good time, sir! You do
not flout, friend, do you?
SERVANT
Not I, sir.
STEPHEN
Not you, sir? You were not best, sir; an' you should, here   100

---

84 *Nor ... gentility* i.e. Nor do I wish you to insist so proudly on your birth into
the rank of gentleman. The argument is conventional, from Seneca and Juvenal
up through the Renaissance Humanists, and class conflicts pervade this play.

87 s.d. SERVANT I.ii begins here in F.

88 *Save you* short for 'God save you', a respectful greeting

90–1 *of a thousand ... land* i.e. who has an annual income of a thousand pounds
from land-rents in Middlesex, from which Stephen (like many country gulls in
Renaissance city comedy) has come to London

93 *simple* a direct inheritor (cf. Dent-S S462.1); but with an inadvertent pun on
another Renaissance meaning, 'foolish', as in 'simpleton'

94 *pretty* considerable in number, quality, or extent (OED)

95 *hard by* close by (OED)

96 *In good time* A common phrase meaning, 'at the right moment' or 'by good
luck', but often expressing ironic acquiescence or amazement (Dent-S TT16); the
Servant may be reacting to Stephen's tactless eagerness for his uncle and cousin
to die, or perhaps merely interrupting so he can deliver his letter promptly.

98 *flout* mock, jeer, insult (OED)

100 *were not best* had better not be

be them can perceive it, and that quickly too; go to. And
they can give it again soundly too an' need be.
SERVANT
Why, sir, let this satisfy you: good faith, I had no such
intent.
STEPHEN
Sir, an' I thought you had, I would talk with you, and that   105
presently.
SERVANT
Good Master Stephen, so you may, sir, at your pleasure.
STEPHEN
And so I would sir, good my saucy companion, an' you
were out o' mine uncle's ground, I can tell you; though I do
not stand upon my gentility neither in't.   110
KNOWELL
Cousin! Cousin! Will this ne'er be left?
STEPHEN
Whoreson base fellow! A mechanical serving-man! By this
cudgel, an't were not for shame, I would –
KNOWELL
What would you do, you peremptory gull?
If you cannot be quiet, get you hence.   115
You see the honest man demeans himself
Modestly towards you, giving no reply
To your unseasoned, quarrelling, rude fashion;
And still you huff it, with a kind of carriage
As void of wit as of humanity.   120
Go, get you in; 'fore heaven, I am ashamed
Thou hast a kinsman's interest in me.   [*Exit* STEPHEN]
SERVANT
I pray you, sir, is this Master Knowell's house?

108–9 *good my ... ground* i.e. my fine impudent fellow! If you weren't on my uncle's
    property (where I have no right to attack his guests) ...
112 *Whoreson* The son of a whore ... but commonly used as a coarse term of ...
    abuse, dislike, or contempt (OED)
    mechanical engaged in manual labour; belonging to the artisan class (OED)
113 *cudgel* a short, thick stick used as a weapon (OED)
    shame i.e. the disgrace of brawling with a social inferior, and perhaps of doing
    so in violation of his uncle's hospitality
114 *peremptory gull* highly gullible but arrogant person
116 *demeans* maintains his demeanour, and/or humbles himself
118 *unseasoned* mistimed, and/or immature
119 *carriage* bearing, manner
122 *interest in me* share of my (family) identity

KNOWELL
  Yes, marry, is it sir.
SERVANT
  I should inquire for a gentleman here, one Master Edward   125
  Knowell; do you know any such, sir, I pray you?
KNOWELL
  I should forget myself else, sir.
SERVANT
  Are you the gentleman? Cry you mercy sir: I was required
  by a gentleman i' the City, as I rode out at this end o' the
  town, to deliver you this letter, sir.   130
KNOWELL
  To me, sir! What do you mean? Pray you, remember your
  court'sy. [Reads] 'To his most selected friend, Master
  Edward Knowell.' What might the gentleman's name be,
  sir, that sent it? Nay, pray you, be covered.
SERVANT
  One Master Wellbred, sir.   135
KNOWELL
  Master Wellbred! A young gentleman, is he not?
SERVANT
  The same, sir; Master Kitely married his sister, the rich mer-
  chant i' the Old Jewry.
KNOWELL
  You say very true. Brainworm!

                    [Enter BRAINWORM]

BRAINWORM
  Sir.   140
KNOWELL
  Make this honest friend drink here; pray you go in.

                    [Exeunt BRAINWORM and SERVANT]

  This letter is directed to my son;
  Yet, I am Edward Knowell too, and may
  With the safe conscience of good manners use

---

124 *marry* a common oath, originally 'by Mary'
127 *I should forget myself else* A common literalizing play on a common phrase
    meaning, forgetting this would be as bad or unlikely as forgetting my own ident-
    ity (cf. *Hamlet*, I.ii.161: 'Horatio – or I do forget myself').
128 *Cry you mercy* I beg your pardon
129 *the City* an old, central, politically independent section of London
131–2 *Pray ... court'sy* Please put your hat back on
138 *Old Jewry* a London street inhabited by Jews until their expulsion in the 13th
    century

The fellow's error to my satisfaction.   145
Well, I will break it ope (old men are curious),
Be it but for the style's sake, and the phrase,
To see if both do answer my son's praises,
Who is, almost, grown the idolater
Of this young Wellbred. What have we here? What's this?   150
[*Reads the letter*] 'Why, Ned, I beseech thee: hast thou for-
sworn all thy friends i' the Old Jewry? Or dost thou think
us all Jews that inhabit there, yet? If thou dost, come over,
and but see our frippery; change an old shirt for a whole
smock with us. Do not conceive that antipathy between us   155
and Hogsden, as was between Jews and hogs' flesh. Leave
thy vigilant father alone to number over his green apricots,
evening and morning, o' the north-west wall; an' I had been
his son, I had saved him the labour, long since; if taking in
all the young wenches that pass by at the back door, and   160
coddling every kernel of the fruit for 'em, would ha' served.
But, prithee, come over to me, quickly, this morning: I have
such a present for thee (our Turkey Company never sent the
like to the Grand Signior)! One is a rhymer, sir, o' your
own batch, your own leaven, but doth think himself Poet-   165
mayor o' the town: willing to be shown, and worthy to be
seen. The other – I will not venture his description with you
till you come, because I would ha' you make hither with an
appetite. If the worst of 'em be not worth your journey,

146–7 *old men … style's sake* Old Knowell tries to justify his impulse to invade his
     son's privacy by deeming it either a symptom of his advanced age or an act of
     disinterested literary criticism.

148 *answer* live up to

153 *yet* still

154 *frippery* a place where cast-off clothes are sold (OED) (see Jonson's *Epigrams*,
     56)

154–5 *change … smock* i.e. trade your old father's company (underwear) for that of
     a healthy wench (whore? virgin?)

157 *number over* count, to see whether any have been stolen

161 *coddling* This plays bawdily on 'cuddling' and 'cod' (as in 'cod-piece'), and on
     the literal meaning, 'stewing' (since 'stew' meant 'prostitute' or 'whorehouse'
     [OED]).
     served sufficed – to save the father the task of counting, and/or to seduce the
     young women

163 *Turkey Company* a chartered group which gave exorbitant presents to the
     Turkish leader in exchange for trading privileges

164–5 *o' your … leaven* i.e. made from the same poetical dough as you

165–6 *Poet-mayor* This term plays on the idea of London's Lord-mayor, and the ety-
     mologically and orthographically similar idea of poet-major.

draw your bill of charges, as unconscionable as any   170
Guildhall verdict will give it you, and you shall be allowed
your *viaticum*.

> *From the Windmill.'*

From the Bordello, it might come as well;
The Spittle; or Pict-hatch. Is this the man   175
My son hath sung so for the happiest wit,
The choicest brain, the times hath sent us forth?
I know not what he may be in the arts,
Nor what in schools; but surely, for his manners,
I judge him a profane and dissolute wretch;   180
Worse, by possession of such great good gifts,
Being the master of so loose a spirit.
Why, what unhallowed ruffian would have writ
In such a scurrilous manner to a friend!
Why should he think I tell my apricots?   185
Or play th' Hesperian dragon with my fruit,
To watch it? Well, my son, I had thought
You'd had more judgement, t'have made election
Of your companions, than t'have ta'en on trust
Such petulant, jeering gamesters, that can spare   190
No argument or subject from their jest.
But I perceive, affection makes a fool
Of any man, too much the father. Brainworm!

[*Enter* BRAINWORM]

BRAINWORM
  Sir.

170-1 *draw ... give it you* Wellbred's letter here ends by joking about Edward suing
  him, with the help of notoriously severe Guildhall juries, if the fools are not
  worth coming to see.
172 *viaticum* travel expenses
173-5 *Windmill ... Pict-Hatch* The return address on Wellbred's letter is the
  Windmill tavern, which stood near the heart of the play's action in the Old
  Jewry, and (according to John Stow's famous Renaissance survey of London)
  had formerly been a synagogue, a monastery, and a nobleman's house
  (Chalfant). Old Knowell complains that the letter could as aptly come from a
  brothel, a hospital for venereal diseases (like the one near Hogsden), or a red-
  light district (like the one near Clerkenwell Green).
176 *happiest* most skilful in performing what the circumstances require; apt, dexter-
  ous, felicitous (OED)
186 *Hesperian dragon* in Greek myth, the guardian of Hera's golden apples
190 *gamesters* gamblers; also, those who indulge in sexual play, especially with
  prostitutes
192-3 *affection ... father* Cf. Jonson's epitaph 'On My First Son'.

KNOWELL

Is the fellow gone that brought this letter?   195

BRAINWORM

Yes, sir, a pretty while since.

KNOWELL

And where's your young master?

BRAINWORM

In his chamber, sir.

KNOWELL

He spake not with the fellow, did he?

BRAINWORM

No, sir, he saw him not.   200

KNOWELL

Take you this letter, and deliver it my son, but with no
notice that I have opened it, on your life.

BRAINWORM

Oh lord, sir, that were a jest indeed!   [*Exit*]

KNOWELL

I am resolved, I will not stop his journey;
Nor practise any violent mean, to stay   205
The unbridled course of youth in him; for that,
Restrained, grows more impatient; and, in kind,
Like to the eager but the generous greyhound,
Who, ne'er so little from his game withheld,
Turns head, and leaps up at his holder's throat.   210
There is a way of winning more by love,
And urging of the modesty, than fear:
Force works on servile natures, not the free.
He that's compelled to goodness, may be good;
But 'tis but for that fit; where others, drawn   215

---

202 *on your life* swear by your life; or, if you value your life
203 *that were a jest indeed* A common expression (Dent-S J41), meaning something
like 'that would be quite a joke', with the implication, 'I would never pull a trick
like that'.
204–18 Old Knowell's soliloquy closely resembles the foster-father's opening soliloquy in Terence's *Adelphoi* (Jackson), and the father's complaints in Plautus's
Trinummus (Carter); the fact that Old Knowell has far less cause for worry than
these precedent fathers may reflect Jonson's undiscriminating assimilation of the
ancients (as critics have assumed), but more likely signals Old Knowell's own
eagerness – despite his professed disdain for literature – to cast himself as the
classic long-suffering parent.
205 *practise ... stay* i.e. use any violent method to restrain
208 *generous* of good breed or stock ... spirited (OED)
209 *n'er ... withheld* i.e. if held back even slightly from its prey
215 *fit* brief crisis

By softness and example, get a habit.
Then, if they stray, but warn 'em: and the same
They should for virtue've done, they'll do for shame.

[*Exit*]

Act I, Scene ii

[*Enter*] EDWARD [*holding a letter*], BRAINWORM

EDWARD
Did he open it, sayest thou?
BRAINWORM
Yes, o' my word, sir, and read the contents.
EDWARD
That scarce contents me. What countenance, prithee, made
he, i' the reading of it? Was he angry, or pleased?
BRAINWORM
Nay sir, I saw him not read it, nor open it, I assure your   5
worship.
EDWARD
No? How know'st thou, then, that he did either?
BRAINWORM
Marry, sir, because he charged me, on my life, to tell
nobody that he opened it; which, unless he had done, he
would never fear to have it revealed.   10
EDWARD
That's true; well, I thank thee, Brainworm.

[*He studies the letter*]

[*Enter* STEPHEN]

STEPHEN
Oh, Brainworm, did'st thou not see a fellow here in a what-
sha'-call-him doublet? He brought mine uncle a letter e'en
now.
BRAINWORM
Yes, Master Stephen, what of him?   15

Act I, Scene ii This is I.iii in F.
  2 *o' my word* i.e. I give you my word that he did
  3 *That scarce contents me* i.e. That's not very pleasant news, it discontents me;
     playing off the other sense of 'contents' in the previous line
 13 *doublet* a close-fitting jacket
 13–14 *e'en now* only moments ago

STEPHEN
 Oh, I ha' such a mind to beat him. Where is he? Canst thou
 tell?
BRAINWORM
 Faith, he is not of that mind: he is gone, Master Stephen.
STEPHEN
 Gone? Which way? When went he? How long since?
BRAINWORM
 He is rid hence. He took horse at the street door.   20
STEPHEN
 And I stayed i' the fields! Whoreson scanderbag rogue! Oh
 that I had but a horse to fetch him back again.
BRAINWORM
 Why, you may ha' my master's gelding, to save your long-
 ing, sir.
STEPHEN
 But I ha' no boots, that's the spite on't.   25
BRAINWORM
 Why, a fine wisp of hay, rolled hard, Master Stephen.
STEPHEN
 No, faith, it's no boot to follow him now: let him e'en go,
 and hang. 'Pray thee, help to truss me a little. He does so
 vex me –
BRAINWORM
 You'll be worse vexed, when you are trussed, Master   30
 Stephen. Best keep unbraced, and walk yourself till you be
 cold: your choler may founder you else.
STEPHEN
 By my faith, and so I will, now thou tell'st me on't. How
 dost thou like my leg, Brainworm?

16 *mind* desire, inclination, determination
21 *i' the fields* i.e. on the side of the house away from the street
   scanderbag rascally (OED); derived from 'Iskanderbeg', 'the patriot chief who
   won the freedom of Albania' in the fifteenth century (H&S)
23–4 *may ha' my ... longing* i.e. have permission to use Old Knowell's castrated
   male horse, to spare you from yearning (cf. Dent-S L422.1) for the means to
   pursue that servant; but with a *double entendre* about Stephen's manliness
26 *fine wisp of hay* a poor man's substitute for riding boots
27 *no boot* no use, with a play on Stephen's bootlessness
28 *truss* tie the 'points' or laces with which the hose were fastened to the doublet
   (OED)
30 *trussed* fastened like the wings or legs of a fowl prepared for cooking (OED) –
   hence, to be gulled, humiliated, possibly hanged
31 *unbraced* unlaced
32 *choler* anger, with a play on 'collar', again suggesting capture or hanging

BRAINWORM
A very good leg, Master Stephen! But the woollen stocking   35
does not commend it so well.
STEPHEN
Foh, the stockings be good enough, now summer is coming
on, for the dust. I'll have a pair of silk again' winter, that I
go to dwell i' the town. I think my leg would show in a silk
hose.   40
BRAINWORM
Believe me, Master Stephen, rarely well.
STEPHEN
In sadness, I think it would: I have a reasonable good leg.
BRAINWORM
You have an excellent good leg, Master Stephen, but I
cannot stay to praise it longer now, and I am very sorry
for't.   45
STEPHEN
Another time will serve, Brainworm. Gramercy for this.

[*Exit* BRAINWORM]

[EDWARD] *laughs having read the letter*

EDWARD
Ha, ha, ha!
STEPHEN
'Slid, I hope, he laughs not at me; an' he do –
EDWARD
Here was a letter, indeed, to be intercepted by a man's
father, and do him good with him! He cannot but think   50
most virtuously, both of me, and the sender, sure; that
make the careful costermonger of him in our 'Familiar
Epistles'. Well, if he read this with patience, I'll be gelt, and
troll ballads for Master John Trundle, yonder, the rest of
my mortality. It is true, and likely, my father may have as   55

---

42 *In sadness* Seriously
46 *Gramercy* Thank you
49 *Here was a letter, indeed* i.e. This was a fine letter. This sentence and the next
   are spoken ironically or sarcastically.
52 *costermonger* seller of fruit in the street, often a term of contempt or abuse
   (OED)
52–3 *'Familiar Epistles'* personal correspondence, as in the classical volumes of
   Epistolae ad Familiares
53–4 *gelt ... yonder* i.e. castrated (like some Italian boys of the period, to preserve
   the high voice) and sing on behalf of a publisher of popular ditties here in
   London

much patience as another man; for he takes much physic,
and oft taking physic makes a man very patient. But would
your packet, Master Wellbred, had arrived at him in such a
minute of his patience; then we had known the end of it,
which now is doubtful, and threatens – [*Sees* STEPHEN]   60
What! My wise cousin! Nay, then, I'll furnish our feast with
one gull more toward the mess. He writes to me of a brace,
and here's one, that's three. Oh, for a fourth; Fortune, if
ever thou'lt use thine eyes, I entreat thee –
STEPHEN
Oh, now I see who he laughed at. He laughed at somebody   65
in that letter. By this good light, an' he had laughed at me –
EDWARD
How now, cousin Stephen, melancholy?
STEPHEN
Yes, a little. I thought you had laughed at me, cousin.
EDWARD
Why, what an' I had, coz, what would you ha' done?
STEPHEN
By this light, I would ha' told mine uncle.   70
EDWARD
Nay, if you would ha' told your uncle, I did laugh at you,
coz.
STEPHEN
Did you, indeed?
EDWARD
Yes, indeed.
STEPHEN
Why, then –
EDWARD   75
What then?
STEPHEN
I am satisfied, it is sufficient.
EDWARD
Why, be so, gentle coz. And, I pray you let me entreat a
courtesy of you. I am sent for, this morning, by a friend i'
the Old Jewry to come to him. It's but crossing over the   80
fields to Moorgate. Will you bear me company? I protest, it

---

62   *mess* a group of four at a meal (cf. Tilley F621)
     brace a pair of game animals, playing again on the trapping of 'gulls'
63   *Fortune* The goddess Fortuna was proverbially blind, but Edward begs her to use
     her eyes for once to help him find a fourth gull.
80   *It's but* i.e. It requires only
81   *Moorgate* a gate in London's City walls leading out into Moorfields

is not to draw you into bond, or any plot against the state,
coz.

STEPHEN

Sir, that's all one, an' 'twere: you shall command me twice
so far as Moorgate to do you good in such a matter. Do you   85
think I would leave you? I protest –

EDWARD

No, no, you shall not protest, coz.

STEPHEN

By my fackins, but I will, by your leave; I'll protest more to
my friend than I'll speak of at this time.

EDWARD

You speak very well, coz.   90

STEPHEN

Nay, not so, neither, you shall pardon me; but I speak to
serve my turn.

EDWARD

Your turn, coz? Do you know what you say? A gentleman
of your sort, parts, carriage, and estimation, to talk o' your
turn i' this company, and to me alone, like a tankard-bearer   95
at a conduit! Fie. A wight that (hitherto) his every step hath
left the stamp of a great foot behind him, as every word the
savour of a strong spirit! And he! This man! So graced,
gilded, or (to use a more fit metaphor) so tin-foiled by
nature, as not ten housewives' pewter (again' a good time)   100
shows more bright to the world than he! And he (as I said
last, so I say again, and still shall say it) – this man! – to
conceal such real ornaments as these, and shadow their
glory, as a milliner's wife does her wrought stomacher, with

82 *bond* confinement, conspiracy, obligation, or agreement to assume debt
84 *that's all one* i.e. that doesn't matter
88 *fackins* faith
92 *turn* purposes (cf. Tilley M139); Edward twists Stephen's word into a reference
    to a 'turn', a single trip to the conduit, by a water-carrier such as Cob
96 *wight* an already archaic (and hence grandiose and poetical) synonym for
    'person'
98 *savour of a strong spirit* reputation for courage, but perhaps playing on mean-
    ings suggesting body odour, which would support some stage-business, perhaps
    involving the old woollen socks the steamed-up Stephen has been wearing
100 *again' a good time* prepared for a holiday celebration (Jackson)
104 *milliner* a vendor of fancy clothing and accessories, especially such as were orig-
    inally imported from Milan (OED)
    stomacher an ornamental covering for the chest (often covered with jewels)
    (OED)

a smoky lawn, or a black cyprus? Oh, coz! It cannot be   105
answered, go not about it. Drake's old ship, at Deptford,
may sooner circle the world again. Come, wrong not the
quality of your desert with looking downward, coz; but
hold up your head, so: and let the Idea of what you are be
portrayed i' your face, that men may read i' your phys-   110
nomy, 'Here, within this place, is to be seen the true, rare,
and accomplished monster, or miracle of nature', which is
all one. What think you of this, coz?
STEPHEN

Why, I do think of it, and I will be more proud, and melancholy, and gentleman-like, than I have been: I'll ensure you.   115
EDWARD

Why, that's resolute Master Stephen! [Aside] Now, if I can
but hold him up to his height, as it is happily begun, it will
do well for a suburb-humour: we may hap have a match
with the City, and play him for forty pound. Come, coz.
STEPHEN

I'll follow you.   120
EDWARD

Follow me? You must go before.
STEPHEN

Nay, an' I must, I will. Pray you, show me, good cousin.

[*Exeunt*]

105 *smoky* of a brownish or bluish shade of grey (OED)
      lawn a kind of fine linen, resembling cambric (OED)
      black cyprus a light transparent material … much used for habiliments of
      mourning (OED). On this and 'lawn', see Jonson's *Epigrams*, 73.
106 *answered, go not about it* i.e. justified, don't bother trying
109 *Idea* the Platonic term for the perfect essence of a thing
110–11 *physnomy* physiognomy, face
117 *height* high degree of any quality (OED), with a suggestion here of haughtiness
118–19 *do well … pound* i.e. provide a worthy example of country foolishness; we
      may even compete with the City version (represented by Matthew), and bet forty
      pounds on Stephen's proving the more ridiculous
118 *match* comparison, contest, or wager
121 *go before* Continuing his flattery of Stephen, Edward insists on the socially
      inferior position of walking behind.

Act I, Scene iii

[Enter] MATTHEW

MATTHEW
I think this be the house: what ho?
COB
[*Within*] Who's there?

[COB *opens the door and enters*]

Oh, Master Matthew! Gi' your worship good morrow.
MATTHEW
What! Cob! How dost thou, good Cob? Dost thou inhabit
here, Cob?   5
COB
Aye, sir, I and my lineage ha' kept a poor house here, in our
days.
MATTHEW
Thy lineage, Monsieur Cob, what lineage? What lineage?
COB
Why, sir, an ancient lineage, and a princely. Mine ance'try
came from a king's belly, no worse man; and yet no man   10
neither (by your worship's leave, I did lie in that) but
Herring the King of fish, from his belly I proceed, one o' the
monarchs o' the world, I assure you. The first red herring
that was broiled in Adam and Eve's kitchen do I fetch my
pedigree from, by the harrots' books. His cob was my   15
great-great-mighty-great grandfather.
MATTHEW
Why mighty? Why mighty, I pray thee?
COB
Oh, it was a mighty while ago, sir, and a mighty great cob.
MATTHEW
How know'st thou that?
COB
How know I? Why, I smell his ghost, ever and anon.   20

Act I, Scene iii This is I.iv in F.
   3 *Gi' your worship good morrow* i.e. Good morning, sir
  12 *Herring the King of fish* In *Lenten Stuffe*, Thomas Nashe calls the herring 'king
     of fishes' (Lever; cf. Tilley, F320). Considering the Prologue's attack on
     Shakespeare's Henry IV plays, and the traces of Falstaff in Bobadill, this phrase
     may also pun on King Henry (or Harry) the Fifth.
  15 *harrots' books* books of heraldry, tracing ancestral nobility; the herring was
     sometimes designated royal because of its 'crowned' head.

MATTHEW

Smell a ghost? Oh unsavoury jest! And the ghost of a
herring, Cob!

COB

Aye, sir, with favour of your worship's nose, Master
Matthew, why not the ghost of a herring-cob, as well as the
ghost of rasher-bacon?   25

MATTHEW

Roger Bacon, thou would'st say?

COB

I say rasher-bacon. They were both broiled o' the coals?
And a man may smell broiled meat, I hope? You are a
scholar: upsolve me that, now.

MATTHEW

Oh raw ignorance! Cob, canst thou show me of a gentle-   30
man, one Captain Bobadill, where his lodging is?

COB

Oh, my guest, sir, you mean!

MATTHEW

Thy guest! Alas! Ha, ha.

COB

Why do you laugh, sir? Do you not mean Captain
Bobadill?   35

MATTHEW

Cob, 'pray thee, advise thyself well: do not wrong the
gentleman, and thyself too. I dare be sworn, he scorns thy
house. He! He lodge in such a base, obscure place, as thy
house! Tut, I know his disposition so well, he would not lie
in thy bed, if thou'dst gi'it him.   40

COB

I will not give it him, though, sir. Mass, I thought somewhat was in't, we could not get him to bed all night! Well,
sir, though he lie not o' my bed, he lies o' my bench: an't
please you to go up, sir, you shall find him with two cush-
ions under his head, and his cloak wrapped about him, as   45
though he had neither won nor lost, and yet, I warrant, he
ne'er cast better in his life than he has done tonight.

MATTHEW

Why? Was he drunk?

---

26 *Roger Bacon* famous thirteenth-century scientist and philosopher; Cob seems to
   believe he was burnt for sorcery

30 *raw* naïve, uneducated, but picking up the metaphor of cooking

41–2 *Mass ... in't* i.e. I swear by the Mass, I knew there had to be some explanation

45–6 *as though ... won nor lost* dazed, expressionless (cf. Tilley L437)

47 *cast* A pun that links throwing dice and throwing up.

COB

Drunk, sir? You hear not me say so. Perhaps he swallowed
a tavern-token, or some such device, sir: I have nothing to   50
do withal. I deal with water, and not with wine. Gi' me my
tankard there, ho! God b'w'you, sir. It's six o'clock: I
should ha' carried two turns, by this. What ho! My stopple!
Come.

MATTHEW

Lie in a water-bearer's house! A gentleman of his havings!   55
Well, I'll tell him my mind.

        [*Enter* TIB, *carrying the tankard and stopple*]

COB

What, Tib, show this gentleman up to the Captain.

        [*Exit* TIB *and* MATTHEW]

Oh, an' my house were the Brazen Head now, faith, it
would e'en speak, 'Mo' fools yet'. You should ha' some
now would take this Master Matthew to be a gentleman, at   60
the least. His father's an honest man, a worshipful fishmonger, and so forth; and now does he creep and wriggle
into acquaintance with all the brave gallants about the
town, such as my guest is (oh, my guest is a fine man), and
they flout him invincibly. He useth every day to a mer-   65
chant's house, where I serve water, one Master Kitely's, i'
the Old Jewry; and here's the jest, he is in love with my
master's sister, Mistress Bridget, and calls her mistress; and
there he will sit you a whole afternoon sometimes, reading
o' these same abominable, vile (a pox on 'em, I cannot   70
abide them) rascally verses, poyetry, poyetry, and speaking
of interludes, 'twill make a man burst to hear him. And the

49–50 *swallowed a tavern-token* Modern editors follow Tilley T79 in making this
a synonym for 'got drunk', but here Cob is wryly offering a polite alternative
explanation for Bobadill's vomiting; probably the slang use derives from Jonson
– who is Tilley's earliest instance – rather than explaining him.

53 *stopple* the plug or stopper for the water-tankard he is late in carrying

55 *havings* manners or possessions

56 s.d. Alternative stagings would have Tib enter earlier with each piece of equip-
ment in turn, or would have her simply throw them in from offstage.

58 *Brazen Head* Roger Bacon was said to have built a brass head that could speak.
See Robert Greene's 1589 play *Friar Bacon and Friar Bungay*, which Jonson
would have known.

65 *invincibly* A 1595 book lists this word as a common malapropism for 'invisibly'
(Jackson).

72 *interludes* already an archaic name for plays

wenches, they do so jeer, and tee-hee at him – well, should
they do so much to me, I'd forswear them all, by the foot
of Pharaoh. There's an oath! How many water-bearers   75
shall you hear swear such an oath? Oh, I have a guest – he
teaches me – he does swear the legiblest, of any man
christ'ned: 'By St. George!' 'The foot of Pharaoh!' 'The
body of me!' 'As I am a gentleman and a soldier!' Such
dainty oaths! And withal, he does take this same filthy   80
roguish tobacco the finest and cleanliest! It would do a man
good to see the fume come forth at's tunnels! Well, he owes
me forty shillings (my wife lent him out of her purse, by sixpence a time) besides his lodging: I would I had it. I shall
ha' it, he says, the next action. Helter skelter, hang sorrow, 85
care'll kill a cat, up-tails all, and a louse for the hangman.

[Exit]

Act I, Scene iv

BOBADILL *is discovered lying on his bench*

BOBADILL
Hostess, hostess.

[Enter TIB*]*

TIB
What say you, sir?

BOBADILL
A cup o' thy small beer, sweet hostess.

TIB
Sir, there's a gentleman, below, would speak with you.

BOBADILL
A gentleman! 'Odso, I am not within.   5

---

82 *tunnels* nostrils

83–4 *sixpence a time* Bobadill has borrowed money from Tib eighty times, and paid
back none.

85 *action* military campaign, with a possible play on 'lawsuit' – the only way Cob
is likely to recover his loan

85–6 *Helter ... hangman* A string of proverbial fragments (Tilley C85, C84; Dent
F210.11), amounting approximately to a shrug of the shoulders.

0 s.d. *discovered* revealed, probably by opening a curtain in front of an area
recessed in the tiring-house façade

3 *small beer* weak beer, considered a treatment for hangover

TIB
My husband told him you were, sir.
BOBADILL
What a plague – what meant he?
MATTHEW
[*Below*] Captain Bobadill?
BOBADILL
Who's there? (Take away the basin, good hostess.) Come
up, sir.   10
TIB
He would desire you to come up, sir.

[*Enter* MATTHEW]

You come into a cleanly house, here.   [*Exit*]
MATTHEW
'Save you, sir. 'Save you, Captain.
BOBADILL
Gentle Master Matthew! Is it you, sir? Please you sit down.
MATTHEW
Thank you, good Captain; you may see, I am somewhat   15
audacious.
BOBADILL
Not so, sir. I was requested to supper last night by a sort of
gallants, where you were wished for, and drunk to, I assure
you.
MATTHEW
Vouchsafe me, by whom, good Captain.   20
BOBADILL
Marry, by young Wellbred, and others. Why, hostess, a
stool here, for this gentleman.
MATTHEW
No haste, sir, 'tis very well.
BOBADILL
Body of me! It was so late ere we parted last night, I can
scarce open my eyes, yet; I was but new risen, as you came.   25
How passes the day abroad, sir? You can tell.
MATTHEW
Faith, some half hour to seven. Now, trust me, you have an
exceeding fine lodging here, very neat, and private!
BOBADILL
Aye, sir; sit down, I pray you. Master Matthew, in any case,

---

12 *cleanly* Probably a reference to some stage-business with the chamber-pot full of
    piss or vomit, and Matthew's reaction to it.
29–31 *in any case, possess ... lodging* i.e. under no circumstances tell any of the
    gentlemen we know where I live

possess no gentleman of our acquaintance with notice of   30
my lodging.

MATTHEW

Who? I sir? No.

BOBADILL

Not that I need to care who know it, for the cabin is convenient, but in regard I would not be too popular, and generally visited, as some are.   35

MATTHEW

True, Captain, I conceive you.

BOBADILL

For, do you see, sir, by the heart of valour in me – except it
be to some peculiar and choice spirits, to whom I am extra-
ordinarily engaged, as yourself, or so – I could not extend
thus far.   40

MATTHEW

Oh Lord, sir, I resolve so.

BOBADILL

I confess, I love a cleanly and quiet privacy, above all the
tumult and roar of fortune. What new book ha' you there?
What! '*Go by, Hieronymo*'?

MATTHEW

Aye, did you ever see it acted? Is't not well penned?   45

BOBADILL

Well penned? I would fain see all the poets of these times
pen such another play as that was! They'll prate and swagger, and keep a stir of art and devices, when (as I am a
gentleman) read 'em, they are the most shallow, pitiful,
barren fellows that live upon the face of the earth, again!   50

MATTHEW

Indeed, here are a number of fine speeches in this book!
'*Oh eyes, no eyes, but fountains fraught with tears*'! There's
a conceit! '*Fountains fraught with tears*'! '*O life, no life, but
lively form of death*'! Another! '*Oh world, no world, but
mass of public wrongs*'! A third! '*Confused and filled with*   55
murder and misdeeds'! A fourth! Oh, the Muses! Is't not

---

33 *cabin* a soldier's tent or temporary shelter

34 *in regard I would not be too popular* i.e. for the sake of avoiding the riff-raff

37–40 *except it be ... thus far* i.e. unless it were to some few admirable characters
     to whom I am deeply indebted, such as you, I would not extend this much
     hospitality

44 '*Go by, Hieronymo*' A famous line from Kyd's *Spanish Tragedy*, here used as a
     synonym for the play; Jonson was hired to write additions to that play a few
     years after writing *Every Man In*, and his Induction to *Bartholomew Fair* (1614)
     makes fun of those who 'swear *Jeronimo* or *Andronicus* are the best plays yet'.

excellent? Is't not simply the best that ever you heard,
Captain? Ha? How do you like it?

BOBADILL

'Tis good.

MATTHEW

[*Reads*] '*To thee, the purest object to my sense,*   60
The most refinèd essence heaven covers,
Send I these lines, wherein I do commence
The happy state of turtle-billing lovers.
If they prove rough, unpolished, harsh and rude,
Haste made the waste. Thus, mildly, I conclude.'   65

BOBADILL *is making him ready all this while*

BOBADILL

Nay, proceed, proceed. Where's this?

MATTHEW

This, sir? A toy o' mine own, in my nonage: the infancy of
my Muses! But when will you come and see my study?
Good faith, I can show you some very good things I have
done of late. That boot becomes your leg passing well,   70
Captain, methinks!

BOBADILL

So, so; it's the fashion gentlemen now use.

MATTHEW

Troth, Captain, an' now you speak o' the fashion, Master
Wellbred's elder brother and I are fall'n out exceedingly.
This other day, I happened to enter into some discourse of   75
a hanger, which I assure you, both for fashion and work-
manship, was most peremptory-beautiful, and gentleman-
like! Yet he condemned and cried it down for the most pied
and ridiculous that ever he saw.

BOBADILL

Squire Downright? The half-brother? Was't not?   80

MATTHEW

Aye, sir, he.

BOBADILL

Hang him, rook, he! Why, he has no more judgement than
a malt-horse. By St. George, I wonder you'd lose a thought

---

63 *turtle-billing* nuzzling like turtle-doves
65 s.d. *making him* getting himself
66 *Where's this* i.e. Where is this poetry taken from?
74 *fall'n out* i.e. fallen out of each other's favour; quarrelling
76 *hanger* decorated loop for holding a sword on the belt
78 *pied* parti-coloured, here probably implying motley or excessively ornate
82 *rook* a crow – here abusive, a variant on 'gull'

upon such an animal: the most peremptory-absurd clown
of Christendom, this day, he is holden. I protest to you, as   85
I am a gentleman and a soldier, I ne'er changed words with
his like. By his discourse, he should eat nothing but hay. He
was born for the manger, pannier, or pack-saddle! He has
not so much as a good phrase in his belly, but all old iron
and rusty proverbs! A good commodity for some smith, to   90
make hobnails of.

MATTHEW

Aye, and he thinks to carry it away with his manhood still,
where he comes. He brags he will gi' me the *bastinado*, as I
hear.

BOBADILL

How! He the *bastinado*! How came he by that word, trow?   95

MATTHEW

Nay, indeed, he said cudgel me; I termed it so for my more
grace.

BOBADILL

That may be: for I was sure, it was none of his word. But,
when? When said he so?

MATTHEW

Faith, yesterday, they say: a young gallant, a friend of mine   100
told me so.

BOBADILL

By the foot of Pharaoh, an' 'twere my case now, I should
send him a *chartel*, presently. The *bastinado*! A most
proper, and sufficient dependence, warranted by the great
Caranza. Come hither. You shall *chartel* him. I'll show you   105
a trick or two you shall kill him with, at pleasure: the first
stoccata, if you will, by this air.

MATTHEW

Indeed, you have absolute knowledge i' the mystery, I have
heard, sir.

---

85 *holden* reputed

91 *hobnails* short nails with large heads used on the soles of heavy boots; hence
   associated with rustic bumpkins (cf. Dent-S H480.1)

92–3 *to carry ... comes* i.e. to get his way (cf. Dent-S C100.1) through manly
   aggressiveness always, wherever he goes

93 *bastinado* a beating with a stick (OED)

102 *an' 'twere my case* i.e. if I were in your situation

103 *chartel* challenge to a duel

103–5 *A most ... Caranza* i.e. An entirely sufficient justification for such a challenge,
   according to the author of a famous book on duelling

107 *stoccata* a thrust or stab with a pointed weapon (OED)

108 *mystery* craft, art (OED)

BOBADILL
Of whom? Of whom ha' you heard it, I beseech you?   110
MATTHEW
Troth, I have heard it spoken of divers, that you have very
rare, and un-in-one-breath-utterable skill, sir.
BOBADILL
By heaven, no, not I; no skill i' the earth: some small rudi-
ments i' the science, as to know my time, distance, or so. I
have professed it more for noblemen and gentlemen's use   115
than mine own practice, I assure you. Hostess, accommodate us with another bed-staff here, quickly.

[Enter TIB]

Lend us another bed-staff.

[Exit TIB]

The woman does not understand the words of action. Look
you, sir. Exalt not your point above this state, at any hand,   120
and let your poniard maintain your defence, thus.

[Enter TIB *with bed-staff]*

Give it to the gentleman, and leave us.

[Exit TIB]

So, sir. Come on. Oh, twine your body more about, that
you may fall to a more sweet comely gentleman-like guard.
So, indifferent. Hollow your body more sir, thus. Now,   125
stand fast o' your left leg, note your distance, keep your due
proportion of time – oh, you disorder your point most
irregularly!
MATTHEW
How is the bearing of it now, sir?
BOBADILL
Oh, out of measure ill! A well-experienced hand would pass   130
upon you, at pleasure.
MATTHEW
How mean you, sir, pass upon me?
BOBADILL
Why, thus, sir (make a thrust at me), come in upon the

111 *divers* various people; like Matthew at l. 21 above, Bobadill seizes on any hint that
      true gallants might actually think well of him, but again names are hard to come by.
117 *bed-staff* a piece of wood used in making up a bed; the next twenty-two lines sus-
      tain a homoerotic *double entendre* that could be emphasized by stage-business
121 *poniard* a short stabbing weapon; a dagger (OED)
130 *out of measure ill* extremely bad

answer, control your point, and make a full career at the
body. The best-practised gallants of the time name it the   135
passada: a most desperate thrust, believe it!

MATTHEW

Well, come, sir.

BOBADILL

Why, you do not manage your weapon with any facility or
grace to invite me: I have no spirit to play with you. Your
dearth of judgement renders you tedious.   140

MATTHEW

But one *venue*, sir.

BOBADILL

Venue! Fie. Most gross denomination, as ever I heard. Oh,
the *stoccata*, while you live, sir. Note that. Come, put on
your cloak, and we'll go to some private place where you
are acquainted, some tavern or so – and have a bit – I'll   145
send for one of these fencers, and he shall breathe you, by
my direction; and then I will teach you your trick. You shall
kill him with it, at the first, if you please. Why, I will learn
you, by the true judgement of the eye, hand, and foot, to
control any enemy's point i' the world. Should your adver-   150
sary confront you with a pistol, 'twere nothing, by this
hand, you should, by the same rule, control his bullet, in a
line; except it were hail-shot, and spread. What money ha'
you about you, Master Matthew?

MATTHEW

Faith, I ha' not past a two shillings, or so.   155

BOBADILL

'Tis somewhat with the least; but, come. We will have a
bunch of radish and salt, to taste our wine; and a pipe of
tobacco, to close the orifice of the stomach; and then we'll
call upon young Wellbred. Perhaps we shall meet the
Corydon, his brother, there, and put him to the question.   160

                                              [*Exeunt*]

---

134 *career* a rapid charge
136 *passada* a forward thrust with the sword, one foot being advanced at the same
     time (OED). Mercutio mocks this terminology in Shakespeare's *Romeo and
     Juliet*, II.iv.26 and III.i.85.
141 *venue* a bout or turn of fencing (OED)
146 *breathe you* exercise you, participate in a training bout; 'breath you' in F
150 *control ... point* deflect or beat down the point of any enemy's sword
156 *'Tis somewhat with the least* i.e. That's rather little (OED somewhat adv. 4)
157 *taste* flavour (OED)
160 *Corydon* traditional name for a shepherd (out of Virgil), hence a rustic boor

Act II, Scene i

[*Enter*] KITELY, CASH [*and*] DOWNRIGHT

KITELY
Thomas, come hither,
There lies a note, within upon my desk;
Here, take my key; it is no matter, neither.
Where is the boy?
CASH   Within, sir, i' the warehouse.
KITELY
Let him tell over, straight, that Spanish gold,   5
And weigh it, with th' pieces of eight. Do you
See the delivery of those silver stuffs,
To Master Lucar. Tell him, if he will,
He shall ha' the grograns, at the rate I told him,
And I will meet him on the Exchange, anon.   10
CASH
Good, sir.   [*Exit*]
KITELY
Do you see that fellow, brother Downright?
DOWNRIGHT
Aye, what of him?
KITELY
He is a jewel, brother.
I took him of a child, up, at my door,   15
And christened him, gave him mine own name, Thomas;
Since bred him at the Hospital; where proving
A toward imp, I called him home, and taught him
So much, as I have made him my cashier,
And given him, who had none, a surname, Cash;   20
And find him in his place so full of faith
That I durst trust my life into his hands.

---

1 This foreshortened verse line leaves room for an actor to establish the hesitations
   that will characterize Kitely.

6 *pieces of eight* Spanish dollars

9 *grograns* coarse fabrics or garments made from them

10 *the Exchange* the Royal Exchange, a gathering place for Elizabethan merchants

15 *took … door* i.e. took him in as a child; this adoption suggests that Kitely's mar-
    riage is sterile, which would help to explain his fear that his wife might desire
    another partner.

17–18 *bred … imp* i.e. paid for his rearing and education at Christ's Hospital (an
    institution for orphans), from which, because he proved to be an eager and
    promising child

DOWNRIGHT
 So would not I in any bastard's, brother –
 As it is like he is – although I knew
 Myself his father. But you said y'had somewhat   25
 To tell me, gentle brother: what is't? What is't?
KITELY
 Faith, I am very loath to utter it,
 As fearing, it may hurt your patience:
 But that I know your judgement is of strength,
 Against the nearness of affection –   30
DOWNRIGHT
 What need this circumstance? Pray you be direct.
KITELY
 I will not say how much I do ascribe
 Unto your friendship; nor, in what regard
 I hold your love; but, let my past behaviour,
 And usage of your sister, but confirm   35
 How well I've been affected to your –
DOWNRIGHT
 You are too tedious, come to the matter, the matter.
KITELY
 Then, without further ceremony, thus.
 My brother Wellbred, sir, I know not how,
 Of late is much declined in what he was,   40
 And greatly altered in his disposition.
 When he came first to lodge here in my house,
 Ne'er trust me if I were not proud of him:
 Methought he bare himself in such a fashion,
 So full of man, and sweetness in his carriage,   45
 And (what was chief) it showed not borrowed in him,
 But all he did became him as his own,
 And seemed as perfect, proper, and possessed
 As breath with life, or colour with the blood.
 But, now, his course is so irregular,   50
 So loose, affected, and deprived of grace,
 And he himself withal so far fall'n off
 From that first place, as scarce no note remains,
 To tell men's judgements where he lately stood.
 He's grown a stranger to all due respect,   55
 Forgetful of his friends, and not content
 To stale himself in all societies,
 He makes my house here common as a mart,
 A theatre, a public receptacle

57 *stale himself* degrade himself, or wear out his welcome, with plays on 'stale' as
  'use a prostitute' and 'urinate'

For giddy humour, and diseased riot;   60
And here (as in a tavern, or a stews)
He and his wild associates spend their hours,
In repetition of lascivious jests;
Swear, leap, drink, dance, and revel night by night;
Control my servants; and indeed what not?   65

DOWNRIGHT

'Sdeynes, I know not what I should say to him, i' the whole
world! He values me at a cracked three-farthings, for aught
I see: it will never out o' the flesh that's bred i' the bone! I
have told him enough, one would think, if that would
serve. But counsel to him is as good as a shoulder of mutton   70
to a sick horse. Well! He knows what to trust to, 'fore
George. Let him spend, and spend, and domineer, till his
heart ache; an' he think to be relieved by me, when he is got
into one o' your City pounds, the Counters, he has the
wrong sow by the ear, i' faith; and claps his dish at the   75
wrong man's door. I'll lay my hand o' my halfpenny ere I
part with't to fetch him out, I'll assure him.

KITELY

Nay, good brother, let it not trouble you thus.

DOWNRIGHT

'Sdeath, he mads me, I could eat my very spur-leathers, for
anger! But why are you so tame? Why do you not speak to   80
him, and tell him how he disquiets your house?

KITELY

Oh, there are divers reasons to dissuade, brother.
But, would yourself vouchsafe to travail in it,
(Though but with plain and easy circumstance),
It would both come much better to his sense,   85

---

61 *stews* brothel
64 *leap* perform feats of gymnastics, a popular form of display-behaviour at the
  time, with associated sexual implications
66 *'Sdeynes* By God's dignity
67 *cracked three-farthings* damaged, low-value Elizabethan coin
68 *it will never . . . the bone* A common proverb (Tilley F365), meaning that he con-
  siders Wellbred incorrigible; Downright's speech degenerates into a series of
  catch-phrases.
70-1 *shoulder . . . horse* i.e. wasted, useless as a cure (also proverbial: Tilley S399,
  C680)
71-2 *'fore George* i.e. I swear before St. George
74-6 *he has the wrong . . . halfpenny* three more proverbs (Tilley S685, D376, H80,
  H315), reiterating his unwillingness to bail Wellbred out
74 *your City pounds, the Counters* London prisons where debtors were held
83 *vouchsafe to travail in it* i.e. consent graciously to work on it

And savour less of stomach, or of passion.
You are his elder brother, and that title
Both gives and warrants you authority;
Which (by your presence seconded) must breed
A kind of duty in him, and regard;   90
Whereas, if I should intimate the least
It would but add contempt to his neglect,
Heap worse on ill, make up a pile of hatred
That, in the rearing, would come tottering down,
And, in the ruin, bury all our love.   95
Nay, more than this, brother, if I should speak
He would be ready from his heat of humour,
And overflowing of the vapour in him,
To blow the ears of his familiars
With the false breath of telling what disgraces,   100
And low disparagements, I had put upon him.
Whilst they, sir, to relieve him in the fable,
Make their loose comments upon every word,
Gesture, or look, I use; mock me all over,
From my flat cap unto my shining shoes;   105
And, out of their impetuous rioting fant'sies,
Beget some slander, that shall dwell with me.
And what would that be, think you? Marry, this:
They would give out – because my wife is fair,
Myself but lately married, and my sister   110
Here sojourning a virgin in my house –
That I were jealous! Nay, as sure as death,
That they would say. And how that I had quarrelled
My brother purposely, thereby to find
An apt pretext to banish them my house.   115
DOWNRIGHT
Mass, perhaps so: they're like enough to do it.
KITELY
Brother, they would, believe it; so should I,

---

86 *stomach* temper, pride, or irritation (OED)
88 *warrants* assures (since primogeniture gives him financial as well as moral authority)
89 *by your presence seconded* i.e. reinforced by your personal qualities, backed up
   by the force of your presence
97–8 *heat … in him* According to humours theory, Wellbred's hostility could be
   explained by an excess of choler, which is hot and dry.
99 *blow the ears of his familiars* i.e. whisper in the ears of his friends
102 *relieve him in the fable* i.e. take a turn at creating this fiction
105 *my flat cap unto my shining shoes* the attire of an ordinary merchant
116 *like* likely

Like one of these penurious quacksalvers,
But set the bills up to mine own disgrace,
And try experiments upon myself;   120
Lend scorn and envy opportunity
To stab my reputation, and good name –

[*Enter*] MATTHEW [*and*] BOBADILL

MATTHEW
I will speak to him –
BOBADILL
Speak to him? Away, by the foot of Pharaoh, you shall not,
you shall not do him that grace. [*To* KITELY] The time of   125
day to you, gentleman o' the house. Is Master Wellbred stir-
ring?
DOWNRIGHT
How then? What should he do?
BOBADILL
[*To* KITELY] Gentleman of the house, it is to you: is he
within, sir?   130
KITELY
He came not to his lodging tonight sir, I assure you.
DOWNRIGHT
[*To* BOBADILL] Why, do you hear? You.
BOBADILL
The gentleman-citizen hath satisfied me, I'll talk to no scav-
enger.

[*Exeunt* MATTHEW *and* BOBADILL]

DOWNRIGHT
How, scavenger? Stay sir, stay.   135
KITELY
Nay, brother Downright. [*Restrains him from following*
BOBADILL]
DOWNRIGHT
'Heart! Stand you away, an' you love me.

---

118 *quacksalvers* quack doctors who travel making ridiculously grandiose claims for
their patent medicines
122 s.d. *Enter* MATTHEW II.ii begins here in F.
133–4 *scavenger* a lowly worker assigned to gather faeces from streets and privies.
When Dickens played Bobadill, 'he went to the back of the stage before he made
his exit ... uttering the last word of the taunt he flings at Downright with a bawl
of stentorian loudness – "Scavenger!" and then darted off the stage at full speed';
Charles and Mary Cowden Clarke, *Recollections of Writers* (1878), quoted in
R. V. Holdsworth, ed., *Every Man in His Humour and The Alchemist: A
Casebook* (London: Macmillan, 1978), p. 138.

KITELY

You shall not follow him now, I pray you, brother, good
faith you shall not: I will overrule you.

DOWNRIGHT

Ha? Scavenger? Well, go to, I say little; but, by this good   140
day (God forgive me I should swear) if I put it up so, say I
am the rankest cow that ever pissed. 'Sdeynes, an' I swal-
low this, I'll ne'er draw my sword in the sight of Fleet Street
again, while I live: I'll sit in a barn, with madge-howlet, and
catch mice first. Scavenger? 'Heart, and I'll go near to fill   145
that huge tumbrel-slop of yours, with somewhat, an' I have
good luck: your Gargantua breech cannot carry it away so.

KITELY

Oh do not fret yourself thus, never think on't.

DOWNRIGHT

These are my brother's consorts, these! These are his com-
rades, his walking mates! He's a gallant, a *Cavaliero* too,   150
right hangman cut! Let me not live, an' I could not find in
my heart to swinge the whole gang of 'em, one after
another, and begin with him first. I am grieved it should be
said he is my brother, and take these courses. Well, as he
brews, so he shall drink, 'fore George, again. Yet, he shall   155
hear on't, and that tightly too, an' I live, i' faith.

---

140 *go to* As at I.i.52, a vague dismissive phrase, here meaning something like the
   modern 'to hell with you' or 'go about your business (unpunished), for now'.
141 *put it up* sheathe it
142 *rankest* most stinking, or most corrupt, perhaps combined as an animal in heat;
   cows were thought to be especially indiscriminate sexually. Downright characteristically associates his virtue with his masculinity.
143 *Fleet Street* a favourite site for street fights
144 *madge-howlet* an owl; perhaps Downright means, become converted from an
   independent predator to a tame domestic animal.
145–7 *'Heart ... so* i.e. I swear by God's heart that I'll put something into those huge
   pants of yours, if I get a chance; your giant breeches aren't going to win so easily.
   Probably he means 'scare the shit out of you': 'somewhat' is clearly a
   euphemism, a 'tumbrel' was often a dung-cart, and the Gargantua reference
   evokes the notorious scatology of Rabelais. Cob apparently suffers the same
   response to terror at III.iv.124 below. Cf. Dent B160.11.
147 *Gargantua* a giant. Jonson actually spells the name 'Garagantua', adding a
   middle 'a', and hence a syllable, to the usual modern form. The longer form was
   not uncommon in the period.
151 *right hangman cut* i.e. perfectly designed for the hangman (who traditionally
   kept the garments of those he executed)
152 *swinge* beat, perhaps hinting also at 'swing', pointing back to 'hangman'
156 *tightly* vigorously (OED)

KITELY
  But, brother, let your reprehension, then,
  Run in an easy current, not o'er-high
  Carried with rashness, or devouring choler;
  But rather use the soft persuading way   160
  Whose powers will work more gently, and compose
  Th' imperfect thoughts you labour to reclaim:
  More winning than enforcing the consent.
DOWNRIGHT
  Aye, aye, let me alone for that, I warrant you.

                    Bell rings

KITELY
  How now? Oh, the bell rings to breakfast.   165
  Brother, I pray you go in, and bear my wife
  Company till I come; I'll but give order
  For some dispatch of business to my servants –

                              [*Exit* DOWNRIGHT]

            [COB] *passes by with his tankard*

  What, Cob? Our maids will have you by the back, i' faith,
  for coming so late this morning.   170
COB
  Perhaps so, sir; take heed somebody have not them by the
  belly, for walking so late in the evening.   [*Exit*]
KITELY
  Well, yet my troubled spirit's somewhat eased,
  Though not reposed in that security
  As I could wish. But I must be content.   175
  Howe'er I set a face on't to the world,
  Would I had lost this finger, at a venture,
  So Wellbred had ne'er lodged within my house.
  Why't cannot be, where there is such resort
  Of wanton gallants, and young revellers,   180
  That any woman should be honest long.

157 *reprehension* rebuke
164 *let me alone for that* i.e. trust me to take care of that
168 s.d. COB *passes by* II.iii begins here in F.
169 *have you by the back* i.e. attack you; this line and Cob's reply are based on a
    proverb: 'The back of a herring ... the belly of a wench are best' (Tilley B11).
    This line and the next were set as verse in F, but neither the length nor the
    rhythm of the lines justifies that setting.
176 *set a face on't* i.e. look comfortable about it, or try to make it look good (Tilley
    F17)

Is't like, that factious beauty will preserve
The public weal of chastity, unshaken,
When such strong motives muster, and make head
Against her single peace? No, no. Beware,   185
When mutual appetite doth meet to treat,
And spirits of one kind, and quality,
Come once to parley, in the pride of blood:
It is no slow conspiracy that follows.
Well, to be plain, if I but thought the time   190
Had answered their affections, all the world
Should not persuade me but I were a cuckold.
Marry, I hope, they ha' not got that start:
For opportunity hath balked 'em yet,
And shall do still, while I have eyes and ears   195
To attend the impositions of my heart.
My presence shall be as an iron bar,
'Twixt the conspiring motions of desire:
Yea, every look or glance mine eye ejects
Shall check occasion, as one doth his slave,   200
When he forgets the limits of prescription.

[*Enter* DAME KITELY *and* BRIDGET]

DAME KITELY
Sister Bridget, pray you fetch down the rosewater above in
the closet.

[*Exit* BRIDGET]

. Sweetheart, will you come in to breakfast?
KITELY
[*Aside*] An' she have overheard me now?   205
DAME KITELY
I pray thee, good muss, we stay for you.

---

182 *factious* tending to provoke conflict
183 *public weal* commonwealth, with the uneasy sense that his domestic treasures
   might be widely shared
184 *make head* mount an army (against that commonwealth), again with anxious,
   bawdy implications
186 *treat* negotiate, reach a treaty
188 *parley* converse, confer; cf. Tilley C122: 'a castle that parleys and a woman that
   hears will both yield'
189 *It is … follows* i.e. a sexual conspiracy quickly results
194 *balked* blocked, stymied
202 *rosewater* water scented with rose petals
206 *muss* term of endearment, possibly from 'mouse'

KITELY
[*Aside*] By heaven I would not for a thousand angels!
DAME KITELY
What ail you sweetheart, are you not well? Speak, good
muss.
KITELY
Troth, my head aches extremely, on a sudden.   210
DAME KITELY
[*Feeling his forehead*] Oh, the Lord!
KITELY
How now? What?
DAME KITELY
Alas, how it burns! Muss, keep you warm; good truth, it is
this new disease! There's a number are troubled withal! For
love's sake, sweetheart, come in, out of the air.   215
KITELY
[*Aside*] How simple, and how subtle are her answers!
A new disease, and many troubled with it!
Why, true: she heard me, all the world to nothing.
DAME KITELY
I pray thee, good sweetheart, come in: the air will do you
harm, in troth.   220
KITELY
[*Aside*] The air! She has me i' the wind! – Sweetheart!
I'll come to you presently: 'twill away, I hope.
DAME KITELY
Pray heaven it do.   [*Exit*]
KITELY
A new disease? I know not, new or old,
But it may well be called poor mortals' plague: 225
For, like a pestilence, it doth infect
The houses of the brain. First, it begins
Solely to work upon the fantasy,

207 *I would not for a thousand angels* i.e. I would rather lose a thousand ten-shilling
   coins (than have had her overhear me)
218 *all the world to nothing* i.e. the whole world could not convince me otherwise
   (Dent-S W865.1)
221 *has me i' the wind* a hunting term, meaning that she has picked up his scent, e.g.
   has caught onto him (cf. Tilley W434); Kitely is thus conceiving himself as a
   horned animal (the cuckold), and may even have misunderstood 'air' and 'heir'.
226–41 *For, like ... shakes me* 'Throughout this speech, Kitely is medically very
   exact in both his description of the brain's anatomy and his understanding of the
   cause, progress, and effects of his disease. Jealousy was considered in current
   medical theory to be a form of melancholy, caused by an excess of choler ...'
   (Jackson).

Filling her seat with such pestiferous air,
As soon corrupts the judgement; and from thence   230
Sends like contagion to the memory,
Still each to other giving the infection.
Which, as a subtle vapour, spreads itself,
Confusedly, through every sensive part,
Till not a thought or motion in the mind,   235
Be free from the black poison of suspect.
Ah, but what misery is it, to know this?
Or, knowing it, to want the mind's erection
In such extremes? Well, I will once more strive
(In spite of this black cloud) myself to be,   240
And shake the fever off, that thus shakes me.   [*Exit*]

Act II, Scene ii

[*Enter*] BRAINWORM [*disguised as a soldier*]

BRAINWORM
'Slid, I cannot choose but laugh, to see myself translated
thus, from a poor creature to a creator; for now must I
create an intolerable sort of lies, or my present profession
loses the grace; and yet the lie to a man of my coat is as
ominous a fruit as the *fico*. Oh sir, it holds for good polity   5
ever, to have that outwardly in vilest estimation, that
inwardly is most dear to us. So much for my borrowed
shape. Well, the troth is, my old master intends to follow
my young, dry foot, over Moorfields to London this morning; now I, knowing of this hunting-match, or rather con-   10

---

229 *pestiferous* tending to produce plague

231 *like* the same kind of

238 *erection* uprightness, solidity of construction, but with puns on (1) sexual
arousal and (2) emergence of (cuckold's) horns – which for Kitely seem
connected

Act II, Scene ii This is II.iv in F.

    4 *grace* something that imparts beauty; an ornament; the part in which the beauty
of a thing consists (OED)

   4–5 *the lie ... fico* i.e. calling a soldier a liar has as dangerous consequences as
making an obscene gesture with the thumb ('the fig')

    5 *polity* policy

    9 *dry foot* to track game by the mere scent of the foot (OED)

  10 *match* contest or appointment

spiracy, and to insinuate with my young master (for so
must we that are blue-waiters, and men of hope and service
do, or perhaps we may wear motley at the year's end, and
who wears motley, you know) have got me afore, in this
disguise, determining here to lie in *ambuscado*, and inter- 15
cept him in the mid-way. If I can but get his cloak, his
purse, his hat, nay, anything, to cut him off, that is, to stay
his journey, *veni, vidi, vici*, I may say with Captain Caesar,
I am made for ever, i' faith. Well, now must I practise to get
the true garb of one of these lance-knights, my arm here, 20
and my

[*Enter* EDWARD *and* STEPHEN]

– young master! And his cousin, Master Stephen, as I am
true counterfeit man of war, and no soldier!
EDWARD
So sir, and how then, coz?
STEPHEN
[*Searching himself*] 'Sfoot, I have lost my purse, I think. 25
EDWARD
How? Lost your purse? Where? When had you it?
STEPHEN
I cannot tell. Stay!
BRAINWORM
'Slid, I am afeared they will know me, would I could get by
them.   [*Moves aside to conceal himself*]
EDWARD
What? Ha' you it? 30
STEPHEN
No, I think I was bewitched, I –
EDWARD
Nay, do not weep the loss, hang it, let it go.

---

11 *insinuate* to win or gain a way for itself into men's minds, favour, or notice
(OED)
12 *blue-waiters* servants, conventionally dressed in blue livery
13–14 *may wear motley ... you know* i.e. may find ourselves in the mixed, coarse
rags of the unemployed, and that's (literally and figuratively) the costume of a
fool; cf. Shakespeare's *As You Like It,* II.vii.34.
15 *ambuscado* ambush
18 *veni, vidi, vici* Julius Caesar's declaration, 'I came, I saw, I conquered'
20 *lance-knights* mercenary foot-soldiers, especially those armed with a lance or
pike (OED)
arm here sword, or possibly a way of simulating a limb maimed in battle

STEPHEN

Oh, it's here: no, an' it had been lost, I had not cared, but
for a jet ring Mistress Mary sent me.

EDWARD

A jet ring? Oh, the posy, the posy?   35

STEPHEN

Fine, i' faith! *'Though fancy sleep, my love is deep.'*
Meaning that though I did not fancy her, yet she loved me
dearly.

EDWARD

Most excellent!

STEPHEN

And then, I sent her another, and my posy was: *'The*   40
deeper, the sweeter, I'll be judged by St. Peter.'

EDWARD

How, by St. Peter? I do not conceive that!

STEPHEN

Marry, St. Peter, to make up the metre.

EDWARD

Well, there the Saint was your good patron, he helped you
at your need: thank him, thank him.   45

[BRAINWORM] *is come back*

BRAINWORM

[*Aside*] I cannot take leave on 'em, so: I will venture, come
what will. [*To* EDWARD *and* STEPHEN] Gentlemen, please
you change a few crowns for a very excellent good blade,
here? I am a poor gentleman, a soldier, one that (in the

---

34 *jet* a black stone, often used for inscribed rings, as in John Donne's lyric 'A Jet
Ring Sent'

35 *posy* short verse motto inscribed within a ring

40-1 *The deeper ... Peter* 'Cf. Barry's *Ram-Alley*, I.i.298–305: "you hold us
widows / but as a pie ... / That hath had many fingers in't before, / ... /Yet says
the proverb, the deeper is the sweeter"' (Jackson). The obvious sexual sense of
this phrase, combined with Edward's inquiry about St. Peter and his possible pun
on 'conceive', makes it tempting to find here an early use of 'Peter' for 'penis'.

43 *make up the metre* i.e. to fill out the poetic line; Stephen seems to have metre and
rhyme confused here, and this weak formalistic justification typifies his willing-
ness to add meaningless flourishes to his speech in order to imitate heroic or
poetical stereotypes.

45 s.d. This odd way of marking an entrance (cf. III.i.21 s.d.) reflects Jonson's pre-
occupation in F with preparing theatre-scripts for the reading public.

46 *venture* make an attempt, take a risk

48 *crowns* coins worth five shillings; Jackson demonstrates that Brainworm's speech
(from here to l. 67) was standard among Elizabethan beggars.

better state of my fortunes) scorned so mean a refuge, but   50
now it is the humour of necessity to have it so. You seem to
be gentlemen, well affected to martial men, else I should
rather die with silence, than live with shame; however,
vouchsafe to remember, it is my want speaks, not myself.
This condition agrees not with my spirit –   55
EDWARD
Where hast thou served?
BRAINWORM
May it please you, sir, in all the late wars of Bohemia,
Hungaria, Dalmatia, Poland, where not, sir? I have been a
poor servitor, by sea and land, any time this fourteen years,
and followed the fortunes of the best commanders in   60
Christendom. I was twice shot at the taking of Aleppo, once
at the relief of Vienna; I have been at Marseilles, Naples,
and the Adriatic gulf, a gentleman-slave in the galleys,
thrice, where I was most dangerously shot in the head,
through both the thighs, and yet, being thus maimed, I am   65
void of maintenance, nothing left me but my scars, the
noted marks of my resolution.
STEPHEN
How will you sell this rapier, friend?
BRAINWORM
Generous sir, I refer it to your own judgement: you are a
gentleman, give me what you please.   70
STEPHEN
True, I am a gentleman, I know that, friend; but what
though? I pray you say, what would you ask?
BRAINWORM
I assure you, the blade may become the side or thigh of the
best prince in Europe.
EDWARD
Aye, with a velvet scabbard, I think.   75
STEPHEN
Nay, an't be mine, it shall have a velvet scabbard, coz,
that's flat: I'd not wear it as 'tis, an' you would give me an
angel.

57–63 *Bohemia . . . gulf* all sites of European battles in the earlier sixteenth century
63 *galleys* low flat-built sea-vessels ... formerly in common use in the
    Mediterranean. The rowers were mostly slaves. (OED)
67 *resolution* unhesitating courageous determination
75 *velvet scabbard* i.e. for decoration rather than use
77 *that's flat* i.e. that's the absolute undeniable truth; a defiant expression of one's
    final resolve or determination (OED; cf. Tilley F345)
78 *angel* an old English gold coin (OED), worth ten shillings

BRAINWORM

At your worship's pleasure, sir: nay, 'tis a most pure
Toledo.   80

STEPHEN

I had rather it were a Spaniard! But tell me, what shall I
give you for it? An' it had a silver hilt –

EDWARD

Come, come, you shall not buy it; [*To* BRAINWORM] hold,
there's a shilling, fellow, take thy rapier.

STEPHEN

Why, but I will buy it now, because you say so, and there's   85
another shilling, fellow. I scorn to be outbidden. What,
shall I walk with a cudgel, like Higginbottom? And may
have a rapier, for money?

EDWARD

You may buy one in the City.

STEPHEN

Tut, I'll buy this i' the field, so I will, I have a mind to't,   90
because 'tis a field rapier. Tell me your lowest price.

EDWARD

You shall not buy it, I say.

STEPHEN

By this money, but I will, though I give more than 'tis
worth.

EDWARD

Come away, you are a fool.   95

STEPHEN

Friend, I am a fool, that's granted: but I'll have it, for that
word's sake. [*To* BRAINWORM] Follow me, for your money.

BRAINWORM

At your service, sir.

[*Exeunt*]

---

80 *Toledo* Swords from Toledo in Spain were renowned for quality; Stephen's reply
suggests that he doesn't realize that Toledo *is* in Spain.

87 *Higginbottom* This person has never been convincingly identified; an example of
how Jonson's love of local reference can make parts of his work inaccessible to
modern audiences.

Act II, Scene iii

[Enter] KNOWELL

KNOWELL

I cannot lose the thought, yet, of this letter
Sent to my son; nor leave t' admire the change
Of manners, and the breeding of our youth,
Within the kingdom, since myself was one.
When I was young, he lived not in the stews   5
Durst have conceived a scorn, and uttered it,
On a grey head: age was authority
Against a buffoon; and a man had, then,
A certain reverence paid unto his years,
That had none due unto his life. So much   10
The sanctity of some prevailed for others.
But, now, we all are fall'n: youth, from their fear;
And age, from that which bred it, good example.
Nay, would ourselves were not the first, even parents,
That did destroy the hopes in our own children;   15
Or they not learned our vices in their cradles,
And sucked in our ill customs with their milk.
Ere all their teeth be born, or they can speak,
We make their palates cunning! The first words
We form their tongues with, are licentious jests!   20
Can it call 'whore'? Cry 'bastard'? Oh, then, kiss it,
A witty child! Can't swear? The father's darling!
Give it two plums. Nay, rather than't shall learn
No bawdy song, the mother herself will teach it!
But this is in the infancy, the days   25
Of the long coat: when it puts on the breeches,

Act II, Scene iii This is II.v in F.

    1–66 *I cannot lose ... mentioned of example* Old Knowell's soliloquy is again
    highly derivative, here drawing primarily on Juvenal's *Satires* (XIII and XIV) and
    Quintillian's *Institutes of Eloquence* (I.1–2), but with traces of Ovid and Horace
    as well (Jackson).

    2 *admire* be amazed by

    5–7 *he lived ... grey head* i.e. not even the young men who lived in brothels would
    have dared disrespect and mock an elder

    13 *it* i.e. fear, respect

    14 *even* Apparently an intensifier, expressing shock that even their own parents
    would thus corrupt children.

    26 *long coat* garment worn by young children of either sex

It will put off all this. Aye, it is like:
When it is gone into the bone already.
No, no: this dye goes deeper than the coat,
Or shirt, or skin. It stains, unto the liver,   30
And heart, in some. And, rather than it should not,
Note what we fathers do! Look how we live!
What mistresses we keep! At what expense,
In our sons' eyes! Where they may handle our gifts,
Hear our lascivious courtships, see our dalliance,   35
Taste of the same provoking meats with us,
To ruin of our states! Nay, when our own
Portion is fled, to prey on their remainder,
We call them into fellowship of vice!
Bait 'em with the young chambermaid, to seal!   40
And teach 'em all bad ways, to buy affection!
This is one path! But there are millions more,
In which we spoil our own with leading them.
Well, I thank heaven, I never yet was he,
That travelled with my son, before sixteen,   45
To show him the Venetian courtesans.
Nor read the grammar of cheating I had made
To my sharp boy, at twelve: repeating still
The rule, 'Get money'; still, 'Get money, boy;
No matter by what means; money will do   50
More, boy, than my Lord's letter'. Neither have I
Dressed snails or mushrooms curiously before him,
Perfumed my sauces, and taught him to make 'em;
Preceding still, with my grey gluttony,
At all the ordinaries; and only feared   55

27 *like* likely (spoken sarcastically)

28 *into the bone* See II.i.68n above.

37–9 *Nay … vice* i.e. Indeed, when we have wasted all our money on these corrupt
      pleasures, we urge our sons to join us, so that we can waste their money too.

40 *seal* i.e. to get them to sign the money away; seal could also mean 'to have sexual
      intercourse' (Williams)

41 *affection* 'affiction' in F. I believe that Lever alone is correct here, in emending to
      'affection' rather than 'affliction', which is plausible but less suitable to the
      specific line of argument, since Knowell is condemning the ways parents buy
      favour from their children and both buy sex from prostitutes.

51 *my Lord's letter* i.e. a recommendation from a powerful aristocrat (Tilley
      M1085); Knowell laments the cynical recognition that capitalism has displaced
      feudalism

52 *Dressed … him* i.e. Served him exotic recipes of snails and mushrooms

54 *Preceding* i.e. Leading the way; possibly an error for 'proceeding'

55 *ordinaries* public eating-houses

His palate should degenerate, not his manners.
These are the trade of fathers, now! However
My son, I hope, hath met within my threshold
None of these household precedents; which are strong
And swift to rape youth to their precipice.   60
But, let the house at home be ne'er so clean –
Swept, or kept sweet from filth; nay, dust, and cobwebs –
If he will live abroad, with his companions,
In dung, and leystalls; it is worth a fear.
Nor is the danger of conversing less   65
Than all that I have mentioned of example.

[*Enter* BRAINWORM, *still disguised*]

BRAINWORM
[*Aside*] My master? Nay, faith, have at you: I am fleshed
now, I have sped so well. [*To* KNOWELL] Worshipful sir, I
beseech you, respect the estate of a poor soldier; I am
ashamed of this base course of life (God's my comfort) but   70
extremity provokes me to't, what remedy?
KNOWELL
I have not for you, now.
BRAINWORM
By the faith I bear unto truth, gentleman, it is no ordinary
custom in me, but only to preserve manhood. I protest to
you, a man I have been, a man I may be, by your sweet   75
bounty.
KNOWELL
'Pray thee, good friend, be satisfied.
BRAINWORM
Good sir, by that hand, you may do the part of a kind
gentleman, in lending a poor soldier the price of two cans
of beer (a matter of small value); the King of heaven shall   80
pay you, and I shall rest thankful; sweet worship –
KNOWELL
Nay, an' you be so importunate –

---

60 *rape ... precipice* i.e. carry young people to the brink of destruction
64 *leystalls* rubbish-dumps
65–6 *Nor is ... of example* An awkward (because necessarily fragmentary) adaptation of Quintilian's warning that immodest conversation among young noblemen can be just as corrupting as conversation with slaves.
67–8 *have at ... so well* i.e. I will attack you, because – having succeeded so well in fooling the last group – I am as charged up and confident as a hunting dog after its first kill
82 *importunate* stubbornly insistent; probably Brainworm is blocking Knowell's way and hanging on his clothes here.

BRAINWORM

Oh, tender sir, need will have his course: I was not made to
this vile use! Well, the edge of the enemy could not have
abated me so much. It's hard when a man hath served in his   85
Prince's cause, and be thus – (*He weeps*) Honourable worship, let me derive a small piece of silver from you, it shall
not be given in the course of time, by this good ground, I
was fain to pawn my rapier last night for a poor supper, I
had sucked the hilts long before, I am a pagan else: sweet   90
honour.

KNOWELL

Believe me, I am taken with some wonder,
To think a fellow of thy outward presence
Should (in the frame and fashion of his mind)
Be so degenerate, and sordid-base!   95
Art thou a man? And sham'st thou not to beg?
To practice such a servile kind of life?
Why, were thy education ne'er so mean,
Having thy limbs, a thousand fairer courses
Offer themselves to thy election.   100
Either the wars might still supply thy wants,
Or service of some virtuous gentleman,
Or honest labour: nay, what can I name,
But would become thee better than to beg?
But men of thy condition feed on sloth,   105
As doth the beetle, on the dung she breeds in,
Not caring how the metal of your minds
Is eaten with the rust of idleness.
Now, afore me, whate'er he be that should
Relieve a person of thy quality,   110
While thou insist's in this loose desperate course,
I would esteem the sin not thine, but his.

BRAINWORM

Faith, sir, I would gladly find some other course, if so –

KNOWELL

Aye, you'd gladly find it, but you will not seek it.

84–5 *the edge ... so much* i.e. enemy swords could never have cast me this low

87–8 *it shall not ... time* i.e. it will eventually be paid back; 'given' is set against
    'derive'

90 *hilts ... else* i.e. handle guards, I swear it's true, as I am a Christian

107 *metal* character, leading into a familiar play on 'mettle'; cf. Tilley I14: 'idleness
    makes the wit rust'

109–12 *afore me ... but his* i.e. I swear, anyone who gives money to someone like
    you, while you insist on living dishonourably as a beggar, is even more respon-
    sible for your misconduct than you are yourself

BRAINWORM
  Alas, sir, where should a man seek? In the wars, there's no   115
  ascent by desert in these days, but – and for service, would
  it were as soon purchased, as wished for (the air's my com-
  fort). I know what I would say –
KNOWELL
  What's thy name?
BRAINWORM
  Please you, Fitzsword, sir.   120
KNOWELL
  Fitzsword?
  Say that a man should entertain thee now,
  Wouldst thou be honest, humble, just, and true?
BRAINWORM
  Sir, by the place and honour of a soldier –
KNOWELL
  Nay, nay, I like not those affected oaths;   125
  Speak plainly man: what thinkst thou of my words?
BRAINWORM
  Nothing, sir, but wish my fortunes were as happy, as my
  service should be honest.
KNOWELL
  Well, follow me, I'll prove thee, if thy deeds
  Will carry a proportion to thy words.   130
BRAINWORM
  Yes sir, straight, I'll but garter my hose.

                                            [*Exit* KNOWELL]

  Oh that my belly were hooped now, for I am ready to burst
  with laughing! Never was bottle or bagpipe fuller. 'Slid,
  was there ever seen a fox in years to betray himself thus?
  Now shall I be possessed of all his counsels; and, by that   135
  conduit, my young master. Well, he is resolved to prove my
  honesty; faith, and I am resolved to prove his patience: oh,
  I shall abuse him intolerably. This small piece of service will

---

117–18 *the air's my comfort* i.e. as a poor homeless man, I must take comfort in the
    air (which costs nothing)
118 *I . . . say* i.e. I could say worse things
120 *Fitzsword* son of the sword
122 *entertain* employ
129, 136, 137 *prove* test
134 *fox in years* clever old creature (cf. Tilley F647); perhaps a play on one of the
    'Reynard the Fox' folktales
135–6 *by that conduit, my young master* i.e. through me, my young master will gain
    access to all his father's plans

bring him clean out of love with the soldier, forever. He
will never come within the sign of it, the sight of a cassock, 140
or a musket-rest again. He will hate the musters at Mile
End for it, to his dying day. It's no matter, let the world
think me a bad counterfeit if I cannot give him the slip, at
an instant; why, this is better than to have stayed his journey! Well, I'll follow him: oh, how I long to be employed. 145

[*Exit*]

Act III, Scene i

[*Enter*] MATTHEW, WELLBRED [*and*] BOBADILL

MATTHEW
Yes, faith, sir, we were at your lodging to seek you, too.
WELLBRED
Oh, I came not there tonight.
BOBADILL
Your brother delivered us as much.
WELLBRED
Who? My brother Downright?
BOBADILL
He. Master Wellbred, I know not in what kind you hold   5
me, but let me say to you this: as sure as honour, I esteem
it so much out of the sunshine of reputation to throw the
least beam of regard upon such a –
WELLBRED
Sir, I must hear no ill words of my brother.
BOBADILL
I protest to you, as I have a thing to be saved about me, I   10
never saw any gentleman-like part –
WELLBRED
Good Captain, faces about, to some other discourse.

---

140 *cassock* soldier's cloak
141–2 *musters at Mile End* militia training sessions at a favourite common
143 *give him the slip* escape from him, with a pun on 'slip' as a counterfeit coin
     (Jackson)

  3 *delivered us* reported to us
  7 *out of the sunshine of reputation* dishonourable
 10 *thing to be saved about me* soul within me
 11 *part* personal quality or attribute (OED)
 12 *faces about* about face, i.e. move in some other direction

BOBADILL
   With your leave, sir, an' there were no more men living
   upon the face of the earth, I should not fancy him, by St.
   George.   15
MATTHEW
   Troth, nor I, he is of a rustical cut, I know not how: he doth
   not carry himself like a gentleman of fashion –
WELLBRED
   Oh, Master Matthew, that's a grace peculiar but to a few:
   quos aequus amavit Jupiter.
MATTHEW
   I understand you sir.   20
WELLBRED
   No question, you do, or you do not, sir.

              [EDWARD] *enters [followed by* STEPHEN]

   Ned Knowell! By my soul welcome; how dost thou, sweet
   spirit, my Genius? 'Slid, I shall love Apollo and the mad
   Thespian girls the better, while I live, for this; my dear
   Fury: now I see there's some love in thee! Sirrah, these be   25
   the two I writ to thee of. Nay, what a drowsy humour is
   this now? Why dost thou not speak?
EDWARD
   Oh, you are a fine gallant, you sent me a rare letter!
WELLBRED
   Why, was't not rare?
EDWARD
   Yes, I'll be sworn, I was ne'er guilty of reading the like: 30
   match it in all Pliny, or Symmachus' epistles, and I'll have

---

16 *of a rustical cut* a crude creation
19 *quos ... Jupiter* those whom impartial Jupiter has loved (Virgil, *Aeneid*, VI, 129)
23 *Genius* tutelary god or attendant spirit (OED)
23–4 *Apollo ... this* i.e. Apollo the sun god (patron of music and poetry) and the
   Muses who frequent the foot of Mount Helicon, for this (Edward's coming to
   see Matthew, or bringing Stephen?)
25 *Fury* an avenging or tormenting infernal spirit (OED); 'dear Fury' alludes to the
   Furies' euphemistic epithet 'Eumenides', or 'kind ones' (Jackson).
28 *gallant* a man of fashion and pleasure; a fine gentleman (OED)
   rare In this exchange, 'rare' means both 'remarkably good or fine' (with irony)
   and 'unusual, uncommon'.
31 *Pliny* the Younger (c. A.D. 61– c. 112), best known for nine books of elegant literary letters on social, political, judicial, and domestic topics
   Symmachus fourth century Roman politician who wrote letters modeled on
   Pliny's style

my judgement burned in the ear for a rogue; make much of
thy vein, for it is inimitable. But I mar'l what camel it was
that had the carriage of it? For doubtless, he was no ordinary beast that brought it!   35

WELLBRED
  Why?

EDWARD
  Why, sayst thou? Why dost thou think that any reasonable
  creature, especially in the morning (the sober time of the
  day too), could have mista'en my father for me?

WELLBRED
  'Slid, you jest, I hope?   40

EDWARD
  Indeed, the best use we can turn it to, is to make a jest on't,
  now; but I'll assure you, my father had the full view o' your
  flourishing style, some hour before I saw it.

WELLBRED
  What a dull slave was this! But, sirrah, what said he to it, i'
  faith?   45

EDWARD
  Nay, I know not what he said; but I have a shrewd guess
  what he thought.

WELLBRED
  What? What?

EDWARD
  Marry, that thou art some strange dissolute young fellow,
  and I a grain or two better, for keeping thee company.   50

WELLBRED
  Tut, that thought is like the moon in her last quarter, 'twill
  change shortly; but, sirrah, I pray thee be acquainted with
  my two hang-bys here. Thou wilt take exceeding pleasure

---

32 *burned ... rogue* i.e. branded on the ear as a vagabond; Jonson's thumb was
    branded for the killing of Gabriel Spencer.
33 *vein* particular strain of talent or genius (OED)
    mar'l marvel
    camel known as a pack animal; figuratively, a great awkward hulking fellow
    (OED)
34 *carriage* task of delivering
34–5 *ordinary* (1) 'usual' (2) 'belonging to the regular staff'. An 'ordinary' was also
    'a courier conveying dispatches or letters at regular intervals', although OED
    does not find this sense until 1667.
43 *flourishing* florid, highly embellished (OED)
50 *a grain ... company* i.e. hardly better, since I spend my time with you
53 *hang-bys* contemptuous term for dependants or hangers-on (OED)

in 'em if thou hear'st 'em once go: my wind instruments. I'll
wind 'em up – but what strange piece of silence is this? The   55
sign of the Dumb Man?

EDWARD

Oh, sir, a kinsman of mine, one that may make your music
the fuller, an' he please: he has his humour, sir.

WELLBRED

Oh, what is't? What is't?

EDWARD

Nay, I'll neither do your judgement nor his folly that   60
wrong, as to prepare your apprehension: I'll leave him to
the mercy o' your search; if you can take him, so.

WELLBRED

Well, Captain Bobadill, Master Matthew, pray you know
this gentleman here, he is a friend of mine, and one that will
deserve your affection. (*To* STEPHEN) I know not your name   65
sir, but I shall be glad of any occasion to render me more
familiar to you.

STEPHEN

My name is Master Stephen, sir, I am this gentleman's own
cousin, sir, his father is mine uncle, sir, I am somewhat
melancholy, but you shall command me, sir, in whatsoever   70
is incident to a gentleman.

BOBADILL

(*To* [EDWARD]) Sir, I must tell you this, I am no general
man, but for Master Wellbred's sake (you may embrace it
at what height of favour you please) I do communicate with
you; and conceive you to be a gentleman of some parts; I   75
love few words.

EDWARD

And I fewer, sir. I have scarce enow to thank you.

54 *go* make their music
   wind-instruments Wellbred may be suggesting a similarity between these fools'
   speech and farting: Shakespeare makes a similar joke concerning 'wind-
   instruments' in *Othello* (III.i.6–11), and Jonson makes a related one later in this
   play (V.i.214). Wellbred's joke depends on the fact that, in Elizabethan usage,
   the noun 'wind' was also pronounced like the modern verb (which appears in the
   next line).

56 *sign ... Man* Wellbred compares the silent Stephen, who is probably striking
   melancholy poses, to the painted sign that would have been hung in front of a
   pub called the Dumb Man.

61 *prepare ... apprehension* prejudice your opinion, spoil the comedy by explaining or exaggerating it

62 *take him, so* discover him, so be it

72 *general man* friendly to everyone

MATTHEW

(*To* STEPHEN) But are you indeed, sir? So given to it?

STEPHEN

Aye, truly, sir, I am mightily given to melancholy.

MATTHEW

Oh, it's your only fine humour, sir, your true melancholy   80
breeds your perfect fine wit, sir: I am melancholy myself
divers times, sir, and then do I no more but take pen and
paper presently, and overflow you half a score, or a dozen
of sonnets, at a sitting.

EDWARD

[*Aside*] Sure, he utters them then, by the gross.   85

STEPHEN

Truly, sir, and I love such things, out of measure.

EDWARD

[*Aside*] I' faith, better than in measure, I'll undertake.

MATTHEW

Why, I pray you, sir, make use of my study, it's at your service.

STEPHEN

I thank you sir, I shall be bold, I warrant you; have you a   90
stool there, to be melancholy upon?

MATTHEW

That I have, sir, and some papers there of mine own doing,
at idle hours, that you'll say there's some sparks of wit in
'em, when you see them.

79–84 *I am mightily ... at a sitting* Both Stephen and Matthew are striking a pose
notoriously popular during this period, and may even seem to be auditioning for
the role of the melancholy romantic scholar-hero Dowsecer in Chapman's *An
Humourous Day's Mirth*, Jonson's immediate precedent in humours-comedy;
but Jonson belittles Chapman by hollowing out this role, and Matthew ends up
looking more like Chapman's Labesha, whose false pose as a man of letters
dooms him as a suitor of women.

80 *your only fine* the finest

85 *utters* Edward plays on the commercial sense, 'puts forth for sale'.
   gross twelve dozen; also, rude, ignorant, stupid

86 *out of measure* beyond all bounds, excessively (OED)

87 *I' faith, better ... measure* i.e. More than you can appreciate good poetic
   rhythm, or metre; only here and at IV.viii.31 (and possibly at V.i.75) does F leave
   a space between the 'I' and the 'faith', so the lines could conceivably be read as
   beginning instead, 'Aye, faith'.

91 *stool* Evidently a stool was the fashionable place for melancholy contemplation,
   but Jonson also plays on the meaning 'toilet'. Q's 'close stool' makes this sense
   more explicit.

WELLBRED

[*Aside*] Would the sparks would kindle once, and become a   95
fire amongst 'em, I might see self-love burnt for her heresy.

STEPHEN

Cousin, is it well? Am I melancholy enough?

EDWARD

Oh, aye, excellent!

WELLBRED

Captain Bobadill: why muse you so?

EDWARD

He is melancholy, too.   100

BOBADILL

Faith, sir, I was thinking of a most honourable piece of service, was performed tomorrow, being St. Mark's day: shall
be some ten years, now.

EDWARD

In what place, Captain?

BOBADILL

Why, at the beleag'ring of Strigonium, where, in less than   105
two hours, seven hundred resolute gentlemen as any were
in Europe lost their lives upon the breach. I'll tell you, gentlemen, it was the first, but the best leaguer, that ever I
beheld, with these eyes, except the taking in of – what do
you call it, last year, by the Genowayes? – but that (of all   110
other) was the most fatal and dangerous exploit that ever I
was ranged in, since I first bore arms before the face of the
enemy, as I am a gentleman, and soldier.

STEPHEN

'So, I had as lief as an angel, I could swear as well as that
gentleman!   115

---

96 *self-love burnt for her heresy* i.e. Matthew's idolatrous personal vanity punished;
   this has an allusive mythological sound to it, but the reference has not been
   identified.

102 *St. Mark's day* April 25. This reinforces the comic impression that the play
   occurs in springtime.

105 *Strigonium* Esztergom, in Hungary; temporarily retaken from the Turks in 1595

107 *breach* a gap in a fortification (OED)

108 *leaguer* siege

110 *Genowayes* Genoese. No such battle is recorded in this uneventful period in
   Genoa's history.

112 *ranged* placed

114 *'So* Another truncated oath, often appearing as 'God so'.

   I ... angel i.e. I wish as much as I wish for a gold coin; but with unwitting irony
   on the juxtaposition of 'angel' and 'swear'

EDWARD

Then, you were a servitor, at both it seems! At Strigonium?
And what-do-you-call't?

BOBADILL

Oh Lord, sir! By St. George, I was the first man that entered
the breach; and, had I not effected it with resolution, I had
been slain, if I had had a million of lives.   120

EDWARD

'Twas pity you had not ten: a cat's, and your own, i' faith.
But, was it possible?

MATTHEW

(*Aside* [*to* STEPHEN]) 'Pray you, mark this discourse, sir.

STEPHEN

(*Aside* [*to* MATTHEW]) So I do.

BOBADILL

I assure you (upon my reputation) 'tis true, and yourself   125
shall confess.

EDWARD

You must bring me to the rack first.

BOBADILL

Observe me judicially, sweet sir: they had planted me three
demi-culverins, just in the mouth of the breach; now, sir (as
we were to give on), their master-gunner (a man of no mean   130
skill and mark, you must think) confronts me with his linstock, ready to give fire; I, spying his intendment, dis-
charged my petronel in his bosom, and with these single

---

116 *servitor* soldier

127 *the rack* an Elizabethan instrument of judicial torture; Edward thus suggests that
he won't easily 'confess' (i.e. acknowledge the truth of) Bobadill's claims.

128 *judicially* judiciously, but picking up the legal metaphors of the previous lines
planted me The 'me' is not the direct object of 'planted', but merely an ethical
dative, and should essentially be ignored for meaning, except as another way
Bobadill indirectly suggests that the entire enemy arsenal was directed against
him personally.

129 *demi-culverins* cannon of about 4½ inches bore (OED)

130 *give on* attack

131 *mark* 'Of mark' means 'noteworthy', with the additional implication here of
marksmanship.

131–2 *linstock* device used to ignite a cannon, consisting of a staff about three feet
long, with a pointed foot to stick in the ground, and a forked head to hold a
lighted match (OED)

133 *petronel* petronel, a kind of large pistol or carbine (OED)

133–4 *these single arms* i.e. merely this slight weapon

arms, my poor rapier, ran violently upon the Moors that
guarded the ordnance, and put 'em pell-mell to the sword.   135
WELLBRED
To the sword? To the rapier, Captain.
EDWARD
Oh, it was a good figure observed, sir! But did you all this,
Captain, without hurting your blade?
BOBADILL
Without any impeach, o' the earth: you shall perceive sir. It
is the most fortunate weapon that ever rid on poor gentle-   140
man's thigh: shall I tell you, sir? You talk of Morglay,
Excalibur, Durindana, or so? Tut, I lend no credit to that is
fabled of 'em, I know the virtue of mine own, and therefore
I dare the boldlier maintain it.
STEPHEN
I mar'l whether it be a Toledo, or no?   145
BOBADILL
A most perfect Toledo, I assure you, sir.
STEPHEN
I have a countryman of his, here.
MATTHEW
Pray you, let's see, sir: yes, faith, it is!
BOBADILL
This a Toledo? Pish.
STEPHEN
Why do you pish, Captain?   150
BOBADILL
A Fleming, by heaven, I'll buy them for a guilder apiece, an'
I would have a thousand of them.
EDWARD
How say you, cousin? I told you thus much?

---

135 *ordnance* i.e. the demi-culverins
137 *figure* i.e. figure of speech
139 *impeach* damage; Bobadill has probably begun flourishing his sword during the
     last part of his previous speech, allowing Edward to see that it appears virtually
     unused – a fact that Bobadill converts, with Falstaff-like aplomb, from an
     exposure of his martial boasting to an extension of it.
141–2 *Morglay ... Durindana* the famous swords of the legendary heroes Sir Bevis
     of Hampton, King Arthur, and Orlando
145 *mar'l* marvel, wonder
149 *Pish* a dismissive noise, like 'pshaw', meaning, 'nonsense'
151 *Fleming* a (cheap) sword made in Flanders; 'the kind of sword issued for the
     fighting in the Low Countries; hence the valuation in Dutch money' (Jackson)
151–2 *I'll buy ... of them* i.e. I could find a thousand of these for no more than a few
     shillings each in the Netherlands

WELLBRED

Where bought you it, Master Stephen?

STEPHEN

Of a scurvy rogue soldier (a hundred of lice go with him),   155
he swore it was a Toledo.

BOBADILL

A poor provant rapier, no better.

MATTHEW

Mass, I think it be, indeed, now I look on't better.

EDWARD

Nay, the longer you look on't, the worse. Put it up, put it
up.   160

STEPHEN

Well, I will put it up, but by – (I ha' forgot the Captain's
oath, I thought to ha' sworn by it) – an' e'er I meet him –

WELLBRED

Oh, it is past help now, sir, you must have patience.

STEPHEN

Whoreson coney-catching rascal! I could eat the very hilts
for anger!   165

EDWARD

A sign of good digestion! You have an ostrich stomach,
cousin.

STEPHEN

A stomach? Would I had him here, you should see an' I had
a stomach.

WELLBRED

It's better as 'tis; come, gentlemen, shall we go?   170

155 *scurvy* sorry, worthless, contemptible (OED); from the literal sense, covered with
     'scurf' or scabs
157 *provant* provided to a soldier; hence, of common or inferior quality (OED)
159 *Put it up* Sheathe it
164 *coney-catching* literally, 'rabbit-catching'; common slang for ensnaring and
     swindling dupes
166 *digestion* Edward implies a second meaning of 'putting up with or bearing with-
     out resistance' (OED does not find this meaning until 1653, but cf. 'swallow this'
     at II.i.142–3).
     ostrich stomach Due to their habit of eating hard substances to assist the gizzard,
     ostriches were presumed able to digest anything, including swords; cf. Tilley I97.
168 *stomach* anger or spirit for fighting; Stephen rejects Edward's possible impli-
     cation that Stephen will 'swallow' anything, tolerate any form of abuse
170 *It's better as 'tis* i.e. It's better not having a fight; but Wellbred may also be sug-
     gesting that they would indeed see the contents of Stephen's stomach if he actu-
     ally had to confront Downright.

[*Enter*] BRAINWORM [*still disguised*]

EDWARD
  A miracle, cousin, look here! Look here!
STEPHEN
  Oh, God's lid, by your leave, do you know me, sir?
BRAINWORM
  Aye sir, I know you, by sight.
STEPHEN
  You sold me a rapier, did you not?
BRAINWORM
  Yes, marry, did I, sir.   175
STEPHEN
  You said it was a Toledo, ha?
BRAINWORM
  True, I did so.
STEPHEN
  But it is none?
BRAINWORM
  No, sir, I confess it, it is none.
STEPHEN
  Do you confess it? Gentlemen, bear witness, he has con-   180
  fessed it. By God's will, an' you had not confessed it –
EDWARD
  Oh cousin, forbear, forbear.
STEPHEN
  Nay, I have done, cousin.
WELLBRED
  Why, you have done like a gentleman, he has confessed it,
  what would you more?   185
STEPHEN
  Yet, by his leave, he is a rascal, under his favour, do you
  see?
EDWARD
  Aye, by his leave, he is, and under favour: a pretty piece of
  civility! [*To* WELLBRED] Sirrah, how dost thou like him?
WELLBRED
  Oh, it's a most precious fool, make much on him; I can   190

170 s.d. *Enter* BRAINWORM III.ii begins here in F.
186 *under ... favour* i.e. if he is willing to agree; as usual, Stephen awkwardly mixes
    belligerence with his mannerly cowardice, here using a phrase that prevents the
    confrontation from authorizing a duel.
190 *make much on him* treat him with courtesy and displays of affection (to encour-
    age more foolishness)

compare him to nothing more happily than a drum: for
everyone may play upon him.

EDWARD

No, no, a child's whistle were far the fitter.

BRAINWORM

Sir, shall I entreat a word with you.

EDWARD

With me, sir? You have not another Toledo to sell, ha' you?   195

BRAINWORM

You are conceited, sir, [*Takes* EDWARD *aside*] your name is
Master Knowell, as I take it?

EDWARD

You are i' the right; you mean not to proceed in the catechism, do you?

BRAINWORM

No, sir, I am none of that coat.   200

EDWARD

Of as bare a coat, though; well, say sir.

BRAINWORM

Faith, sir, I am but servant to the drum extraordinary, and
indeed (this smoky varnish being washed off, and three or
four patches removed) I appear your worship's in reversion,
after the decease of your good father: Brainworm.   205

EDWARD

Brainworm! 'Slight, what breath of a conjurer hath blown
thee hither in this shape?

BRAINWORM

The breath o' your letter, sir, this morning: the same that
blew you to the Windmill, and your father after you.

EDWARD

My father?   210

---

191 *happily* fittingly

196 *conceited* clever, witty, amusing (OED)

198–9 *catechism* The Child's Catechism (used at confirmation) in the 1549 Book of
    Common Prayer begins: 'What is your name? ... Who gave you this name?'
    (Jackson).

200 *none ... coat* i.e. not a clergyman

202 *servant to the drum extraordinary* a soldier not belonging to the regular ranks,
    temporarily employed for a special purpose

203 *smoky varnish* dark, dusky coating, with sense of 'disguise'

204 *in reversion* conditional upon ... the death of a person (OED); Edward will
    inherit the estate of Old Knowell, and hence Brainworm as his servant.

206–7 *'Slight ... shape?* i.e. By God's light, what magic spell has transported and
    transformed you? Cf. Tilley W441: 'what wind blows you hither'?

BRAINWORM

Nay, never start, 'tis true, he has followed you over the fields, by the foot, as you would do a hare i' the snow.

EDWARD

Sirrah, Wellbred, what shall we do, sirrah? My father is come over, after me.

WELLBRED

Thy father? Where is he?   215

BRAINWORM

At Justice Clement's house here in Coleman Street, where he but stays my return; and then –

WELLBRED

Who's this? Brainworm?

BRAINWORM

The same, sir.

WELLBRED

Why how, i' the name of wit, com'st thou transmuted thus?   220

BRAINWORM

Faith, a device, a device; nay, for the love of reason, gentlemen, and avoiding the danger, stand not here, withdraw, and I'll tell you all.

WELLBRED

But, art thou sure he will stay thy return?

BRAINWORM

Do I live, sir? What a question is that?   225

WELLBRED

We'll prorogue his expectation, then, a little: Brainworm, thou shalt go with us. Come on, gentlemen, nay, I pray thee, sweet Ned, droop not: 'heart, an' our wits be so wretchedly dull that one old plodding brain can outstrip us all, would we were e'en pressed to make porters of; and   230 serve out the remnant of our days in Thames Street, or at Custom House quay, in a civil war against the carmen.

BRAINWORM

Amen, amen, amen, say I.

[*Exeunt*]

217 *but stays* waits only for
221 *device* plot, stratagem (OED)
226 *prorogue ... expectation* prolong his waiting
230 *would we ... porters of* i.e. then I wish we were all compelled to work as porters; Wellbred is saying that if they can't outwit Edward's father, they deserve this fate.
232 *civil war against the carmen* Porters (who carried by hand) and carmen (using carts) competed fiercely for the business of carrying goods in from the Thames.

Act III, Scene ii

[Enter] KITELY [and] CASH

KITELY
What says he, Thomas? Did you speak with him?
CASH
He will expect you, sir, within this half hour.
KITELY
Has he the money ready, can you tell?
CASH
Yes, sir, the money was brought in last night.
KITELY
Oh, that's well; fetch me my cloak, my cloak.   5

[*Exit* CASH]

Stay, let me see, an hour, to go and come;
Aye, that will be the least; and then 'twill be
An hour before I can dispatch with him;
Or very near: well, I will say two hours.
Two hours? Ha? Things never dreamed of yet   10
May be contrived, aye, and effected too,
In two hours' absence; well, I will not go.
Two hours: no, fleering opportunity,
I will not give your subtlety that scope.
Who will not judge him worthy to be robbed,   15
That sets his doors wide open to a thief,
And shows the felon where his treasure lies?
Again, what earthy spirit but will attempt
To taste the fruit of beauty's golden tree,
When leaden sleep seals up the dragon's eyes?   20
I will not go. Business, go by, for once.
No, beauty, no: you are of too good caract,
To be left so, without a guard, or open!
Your lustre too'll inflame, at any distance,
Draw courtship to you, as a jet doth straws,   25
Put motion in a stone, strike fire from ice,

Act III, Scene ii This is III.iii in F.

13 *fleering* laughing mockingly

18–20 *what earthy ... dragon's eyes* See I.i.186–7 and n.

22 *caract* carat; also, figuratively, worth, value, estimate (OED)

25 *jet* a black stone that attracts light bodies when electrified by rubbing; cf. Dent
   J49.00

26 *Put motion ... ice* These were proverbs for impossibility (Tilley S879, F284).

Nay, make a porter leap you, with his burden!
You must be then kept up, close, and well-watched,
For, give you opportunity, no quicksand
Devours or swallows swifter! He that lends   30
His wife (if she be fair) or time, or place,
Compels her to be false. I will not go.
The dangers are too many. And, then, the dressing
Is a most main attractive! Our great heads,
Within the City, never were in safety,   35
Since our wives wore these little caps: I'll change 'em,
I'll change 'em straight, in mine. Mine shall no more
Wear three-piled acorns, to make my horns ache.
Nor will I go. I am resolved for that.

[Enter CASH, *with cloak]*

Carry in my cloak again. Yet, stay. Yet, do, too.   40
I will defer going, on all occasions.
CASH
Sir. Snare, your scrivener, will be there with th' bonds.
KITELY
That's true! Fool on me! I had clean forgot it,
I must go. What's o'clock?
CASH   Exchange time, sir.

---

27 *leap* perform feats of gymnastics, or sexually assault. Cf. II.i.64, and Iago's
    intransitive usage: 'I do suspect the lusty Moor / Hath leaped into my seat'
    (*Othello* II.i.295–6). In referring to a porter, Kitely unwittingly echoes Well-
    bred's last speech of the preceding scene.
    with his burden i.e. even while carrying his load, but with a suggestion also of
    sexual erection and the seminal load; 'burden' was also a term for the foetus in
    the womb.
34 *most main attractive* powerful attraction
34–6 *Our great heads ... little caps* i.e. The head men of London have not been safe
    (from having their heads sprout cuckolds' horns) since women started wearing
    the fashionable little hats
37 *straight* straightaway, immediately (OED)
38 *three-piled acorns* small caps shaped like the cup of an acorn, made of velvet
    having a triply dense nap. A velvet-like fur covers the new antlers of a stag,
    common symbol of the cuckold.
    make ... ache Referring to the pain of growing cuckold's horns, the phrase sug-
    gest a pun on 'ache-horns'.
42 *scrivener* here a notary, a person publicly authorized to draw up or attest con-
    tracts or similar documents (OED)
44 *Exchange time* i.e. opening time of the Exchange (thought to be 10 AM); see
    II.i.10

KITELY

[*Aside*] 'Heart, then will Wellbred presently be here, too,   45
With one or other of his loose consorts.
I am a knave if I know what to say,
What course to take, or which way to resolve.
My brain (methinks) is like an hourglass,
Wherein my 'maginations run like sands,   50
Filling up time; but then are turned, and turned;
So that I know not what to stay upon,
And less, to put in act. It shall be so.
Nay, I dare build upon his secrecy,
He knows not to deceive me. Thomas?

CASH   Sir.   55

KITELY

[*Aside*] Yet now I have bethought me, too, I will not.
Thomas, is Cob within?

CASH   I think he be, sir.

KITELY

[*Aside*] But he'll prate too, there's no speech of him.
No, there were no man o' the earth to Thomas,
If I durst trust him; there is all the doubt.   60
But, should he have a chink in him, I were gone,
Lost i' my fame for ever: talk for th' Exchange.
The manner he hath stood with, till this present,
Doth promise no such change! What should I fear then?
Well, come what will, I'll tempt my fortune, once.   65
Thomas – you may deceive me, but, I hope –
Your love, to me, is more –

CASH   Sir, if a servant's
Duty, with faith, may be called love, you are
More than in hope, you are possessed of it.

KITELY

I thank you, heartily, Thomas; gi' me your hand;   70
With all my heart, good Thomas. I have, Thomas,

---

47 *I am a knave if* One version of a common colloquialism ('I'll be damned if')
   meaning 'I surely don't' or 'I surely won't' (cf. Dent-S J49.1: 'I am a jew else').

52–3 *know ... act* do not know what I should pause over, and know even less what
   I should act on

54 *build upon* i.e. have faith in

58 *there's no speech of him* i.e. it wouldn't do to speak to him

61 *chink* crack, leak

66 *Thomas – you may deceive* ... Kitely's vacillating conversation with Cash over
   the next 79 lines is persistently similar (as editors beginning with William
   Gifford in 1816 have noted) to King John's conversation with Hubert in III.iii of
   Shakespeare's *King John* (probably 1595–96).

A secret to impart unto you – but
When once you have it, I must seal your lips up:
So far I tell you, Thomas.
CASH   Sir, for that –
KITELY
Nay, hear me out. Think I esteem you, Thomas,   75
When I will let you in, thus, to my private.
It is a thing sits nearer to my crest
Than thou art ware of, Thomas. If thou should'st
Reveal it, but –
CASH   How? I reveal it?
KITELY   Nay,
I do not think thou would'st; but if thou should'st: 80
'Twere a great weakness.
CASH   A great treachery.
Give it no other name.
KITELY   Thou wilt not do't, then?
CASH
Sir, if I do, mankind disclaim me, ever.
KITELY
[*Aside*] He will not swear, he has some reservation,
Some concealed purpose, and close meaning, sure;   85
Else (being urged so much) how should he choose
But lend an oath to all this protestation?
He's no precisian, that I am certain of.
Nor rigid Roman Catholic. He'll play
At Fayles, and Tick-tack, I have heard him swear.   90
What should I think of it? Urge him again,
And by some other way? I will do so.
Well, Thomas, thou hast sworn not to disclose;
Yes, you did swear?

76 *private* private or personal matter (OED); also 'private parts', as the next line
    suggests
77 *crest* heraldic device representing a noble house; hence, reputation. Since a crest
    was originally worn on a knight's helmet, Kitely alludes here – again – to the
    cuckold's horns; but the word could also mean 'penis' (Williams); see II.i.238n.
83 *mankind ... ever* i.e. may the human race disown me forever
88 *precisian* one who is precise in religious observance: ... synonymous with
    Puritan (OED). Kitely thus feels he cannot explain away Thomas's failure to
    swear an oath of loyalty, as he could if Thomas were like the Puritans on the one
    side and the Catholics on the other in refusing to take the Elizabethan oath of
    allegiance.
90 *Fayles, and Tick-tack* forms of backgammon, in which dice are thrown to deter-
    mine moves. Puritans and 'rigid' Roman Catholics abjured games of chance as
    well as swearing of oaths.

CASH   Not yet, sir, but I will,
  Please you –
KITELY   No, Thomas, I dare take thy word.   95
  But; if thou wilt swear, do, as thou think'st good;
  I am resolved without it; at thy pleasure.
CASH
  By my soul's safety then, sir, I protest.
  My tongue shall ne'er take knowledge of a word
  Delivered me in nature of your trust.   100
KITELY
  It's too much, these ceremonies need not,
  I know thy faith to be as firm as rock.
  Thomas, come hither, near: we cannot be
  Too private, in this business. So it is –
  [*Aside*] Now he has sworn, I dare the safelier venture –   105
  I have of late, by divers observations –
  [*Aside*] But whether his oath can bind him, yea or no,
  Being not taken lawfully? Ha? Say you?
  I will ask counsel, ere I do proceed –
  Thomas, it will be now too late to stay,   110
  I'll spy some fitter time soon, or tomorrow.
CASH
  Sir, at your pleasure.
KITELY   I will think. And, Thomas,
  I pray you search the books 'gainst my return,
  For the receipts 'twixt me and Traps.
CASH   I will, sir.
KITELY
  And, hear you, if your mistress' brother, Wellbred,   115
  Chance to bring hither any gentlemen
  Ere I come back: let one straight bring me word.
CASH
  Very well, sir.
KITELY   To the Exchange; do you hear?
  Or here in Coleman Street, to Justice Clement's.
  Forget it not, nor be not out of the way.   120
CASH
  I will not, sir.
KITELY   I pray you have a care on't.
  Or whether he come or no, if any other,
  Stranger or else, fail not to send me word.

---

98 *protest* assert in formal or solemn terms (OED)

101 *need not* are not necessary

108 *Say you?* i.e. What do you say? Probably addressed to the audience.

120 *nor be not out of the way* i.e. and never leave them alone here

CASH
  I shall not, sir.
KITELY   Be't your special business
  Now, to remember it.
CASH   Sir. I warrant you.   125
KITELY
  But, Thomas, this is not the secret, Thomas,
  I told you of.
CASH   No, sir. I do suppose it.
KITELY
  Believe me, it is not.
CASH   Sir. I do believe you.
KITELY
  By heaven, it is not, that's enough. But, Thomas,
  I would not you should utter it, do you see,   130
  To any creature living, yet, I care not.
  Well, I must hence. Thomas, conceive thus much.
  It was a trial of you, when I meant
  So deep a secret to you, I mean not this,
  But that I have to tell you, this is nothing, this.   135
  But, Thomas, keep this from my wife, I charge you,
  Locked up in silence, midnight, buried here.
  [*Aside*] No greater hell, than to be slave to fear.   [*Exit*]
CASH
  'Locked up in silence, midnight, buried here'.
  Whence should this flood of passion (trow) take head? Ha?   140
  Best dream no longer of this running humour,
  For fear I sink! The violence of the stream
  Already hath transported me so far,
  That I can feel no ground at all! But soft,
  Oh, 'tis our water-bearer: somewhat has crossed him, now.   145

                    [*Enter*] COB

133–5 *It was ... nothing, this* i.e. I was testing you for another time when I will tell
    you the truly deep secret – not this assignment of informing me about men visit-
    ing my wife, but the real secret; this one is trivial
140 *take head* have its source (like a river), but also carrying on the theme of heads,
    whether sprouting fantasies or cuckold's horns
141 *running humour* i.e. Kitely's passionate mood
145 s.d. *Enter* COB III.iv begins here in F.

COB

Fasting days? What would you tell me of fasting days?
'Slid, would they were all on a light fire for me. They say,
the whole world shall be consumed with fire one day, but
would I had these Ember-weeks and villainous Fridays
burnt, in the meantime, and then –   150

CASH

Why, how now, Cob, what moves thee to this choler? Ha?

COB

Collar, Master Thomas? I scorn your collar, I sir, I am none
o' your cart-horse, though I carry, and draw water. An' you
offer to ride me, with your collar, or halter either, I may
hap show you a jade's trick, sir.   155

CASH

Oh, you'll slip your head out of the collar? Why, goodman
Cob, you mistake me.

COB

Nay, I have my rheum, and I can be angry as well as
another, sir.

CASH

Thy rheum, Cob? Thy humour, thy humour! Thou mis- 160
tak'st.

COB

Humour? Mack, I think it be so, indeed; what is that
humour? Some rare thing, I warrant.

CASH

Marry, I'll tell thee, Cob: it is a gentleman-like monster,

---

146 *fasting days* Fridays, Saturdays, Ember days (see l. 149n below), holy day eves,
and Lent, when selling or eating meat was forbidden. Fasting days were 'a very
unpopular relic of pre-Reformation days, adhered to by the Government for
economic rather than religious reasons; the Government claimed that this helped
the English fishing industry' (Seymour-Smith).

147 *on a light fire* in a blaze (OED light *a.*²)

149 *Ember-weeks* weeks during which fasts are observed on Wednesday and the following Friday and Saturday; there are four such weeks annually, one in each
season. Cob plays on 'ember' in the sense of smouldering wood or coal, but its
etymology as a term of religious practice is uncertain.

151 *choler* anger; also the humour that produces anger

154 *ride* oppress or harass; tyrannize over (OED), with the underlying sense of using
someone as a horse

155 *jade's trick* behaviour of an ill-tempered draught horse; cf. Dent-S J29.1

158 *rheum* an outmoded term for 'humour'

162 *Mack* an exclamation, probably an oath derived from either 'by Mary' or 'by the
Mass'

bred, in the special gallantry of our time, by affectation; 165
and fed by folly.

COB

How? Must it be fed?

CASH

Oh, aye, humour is nothing, if it be not fed. Didst thou
never hear that? It's a common phrase, 'Feed my humour'.

COB

I'll none on it: humour, avaunt, I know you not, begone. 170
Let who will make hungry meals for your monstership, it
shall not be I. Feed you, quoth he? 'Slid, I ha' much ado to
feed myself; especially on these lean rascally days, too; an't
had been any other day but a fasting day (a plague on them
all for me), by this light, one might have done the com- 175
monwealth good service, and have drowned them all i' the
flood, two or three hundred thousand years ago. Oh, I do
stomach them hugely! I have a maw now, an' 'twere for Sir
Bevis his horse, against 'em.

CASH

I pray thee, good Cob, what makes thee so out of love with 180
fasting days?

COB

Marry, that which will make any man out of love with 'em,
I think: their bad conditions, an' you will needs know.
First, they are of a Flemish breed, I am sure on't, for they
ravin up more butter than all the days of the week beside; 185
next, they stink of fish and leek-porridge miserably; thirdly,
they'll keep a man devoutly hungry all day, and at night
send him supperless to bed.

---

169 *Feed my humour* i.e. Indulge my whim or mood; cf. Dent-S H806.1
170 *avaunt* begone
171 *make hungry meals for your monstership* i.e. feed that monstrous, all-consuming
humour; or possibly, go hungry in order to save for that task
173 *rascally* wretched, miserable, mean (OED)
175 *by this light* i.e. I swear by this heavenly light
178 *stomach them hugely* i.e. resent them greatly, with a punning reference to hunger
maw stomach, mouth, or jaws; hence, appetite (OED)
178-9 *I ... horse* i.e. I'm so hungry for revenge on these fasting days, I could eat Sir
Bevis's horse (named Arundel; see III.i.141–2n.) – which would violate the
restriction against eating meat
183 *an' you will needs know* i.e. if you insist on knowing
184 *Flemish* Citizens of Flanders were notorious for their love of butter; Jackson
finds a (literally humorous) pun on 'phlegm-ish', noting that eating fish was
thought to generate phlegm.
185 *ravin up* devour

CASH

Indeed, these are faults, Cob.

COB

Nay, an' this were all, 'twere something, but they are the   190
only known enemies to my generation. A fasting day no
sooner comes, but my lineage goes to rack, poor cobs, they
smoke for it, they are made martyrs o' the gridiron, they
melt in passion; and your maids too know this, and yet
would have me turn Hannibal, and eat my own fish and   195
blood. (*He pulls out a red herring*) My princely coz, fear
nothing: I have not the heart to devour you, an' I might be
made as rich as King Cophetua. Oh, that I had room for my
tears, I could weep salt water enough, now, to preserve the
lives of ten thousand of my kin. But I may curse none but   200
these filthy almanacs, for an't were not for them, these days
of persecution would ne'er be known. I'll be hanged, an'
some fishmonger's son do not make of 'em; and puts in
more fasting days than he should do, because he would
utter his father's dried stock-fish, and stinking conger.   205

CASH

'Slight, peace, thou'lt be beaten like a stock-fish, else: here

---

191 *generation* family, breed (OED)

192 *my lineage* i.e. as a cob, or head of a herring; see I.iii.6–16

    rack a set of bars supporting a cooking spit (OED); also, a common Renaissance
    instrument of torture; the two meanings conjoin for fish being cooked

193 *smoke for it* i.e. suffer severely as a consequence (originally, as also here, with
    reference to actual burning)

    martyrs o' the gridiron like St. Lawrence, who, according to tradition, was put
    to death in this manner in A.D. 258

195 *Hannibal* The name of the Carthaginian general (247–182 B.C.) is Cob's mistake
    for 'cannibal'.

198 *King Cophetua* 'A song of a Beggar and a King', in Richard Johnson's 1612
    ballad collection *A Crowne-Garland of Goulden Roses* (sigs. D4r–D6r), suggests
    that this legendary African monarch was known for his wealth.

201 *almanacs* popular annual books containing a calendar, astronomical data, and
    ecclesiastical and other anniversaries

203 *some fishmonger's son* This may be simply a joke about the profitability for fish-
    sellers of 'fish-days', but (as Jackson points out) possibly also a risky joke against
    the powerful politician William Cecil, who instituted 'Cecil's Fast' (as the
    Wednesday fish-day was known) and was often accused of coming from too
    lowly a family to justify his exalted position in Queen Elizabeth's court.

205 *utter* sell; see III.i.85n.

    stock-fish dried cod that was beaten before cooking; cf. Tilley S867

    conger a salt-water eel, six to ten feet in length

is Master Matthew. Now must I look out for a messenger
to my master.

                                                    [*Exeunt*]

Act III, Scene iii

[*Enter*] WELLBRED, EDWARD, BRAINWORM, BOBADILL,
              MATTHEW [*and*] STEPHEN

WELLBRED
Beshrew me, but it was an absolute good jest, and exceed-
ingly well carried!
EDWARD
Aye, and our ignorance maintained it as well, did it not?
WELLBRED
Yes, faith, but was't possible thou should'st not know him?
I forgive Master Stephen, for he is stupidity itself!   5
EDWARD
'Fore God, not I, an' I might have been joined patent with
one of the seven wise masters for knowing him. He had so
writhen himself into the habit of one of your poor infantry,
your decayed, ruinous, worm-eaten gentlemen of the
round: such as have vowed to sit on the skirts of the City,   10
let your Provost and his half-dozen of halberdiers do what

Act III, Scene iii This is III.v in F.

  1 *Beshrew me, but it was* i.e. Curse me if it was not
  6 *joined patent* sharing by letters patent (open letters from a person in authority)
    in some privilege or office (OED)
  7 *seven wise masters* the seven Roman philosophers, tutors to Diocletian's son,
    who saved their student from his stepmother's malicious designs by an elaborate
    plan that involved telling nightly stories to the Emperor; or possibly the Seven
    Sages of ancient Greece
  8 *writhen ... habit* i.e. contorted (with a pun on 'written' enabled by Elizabethan
    pronunciation) himself into the 'attire characteristic of a particular ... profes-
    sion', and implicitly into the behaviour as well
  9–10 *gentlemen of the round* members of a watch, which goes round a camp or
    the ramparts of a fortress, etc., or which parades the streets of a town to preserve
    good order (OED); here their 'circuit' has become the outskirts of London and
    their occupation, begging.
  11 *Provost* an officer charged with the apprehension, custody, and punishment of
    offenders (OED); Elizabeth issued severe edicts against such beggars in 1598.
    halberdiers members of a civic guard carrying halberds as a badge of office; a halberd
    was a combination of spear and battle-axe, consisting of a sharp-edged blade ending
    in a point, and a spear-head, mounted on a handle five to seven feet long (OED)

they can; and have translated begging out of the old hackney pace, to a fine easy amble, and made it run as smooth
of the tongue as a shove-groat shilling. Into the likeness of
one of these *reformados* had he moulded himself so per-   15
fectly, observing every trick of their action, as varying the
accent, swearing with an emphasis, indeed all, with so
special and exquisite a grace that (hadst thou seen him)
thou wouldst have sworn he might have been sergeant-
major, if not lieutenant-colonel, to the regiment.   20

WELLBRED
Why, Brainworm, who would have thought thou hadst
been such an artificer?

EDWARD
An artificer? An architect! Except a man had studied begging all his lifetime, and been a weaver of language, from
his infancy, for the clothing of it, I never saw his rival!   25

WELLBRED
Where got'st thou this coat, I mar'l?

BRAINWORM
Of a Houndsditch man, sir. One of the devil's near kins-
men, a broker.

WELLBRED
That cannot be, if the proverb hold; for, a crafty knave
needs no broker.   30

BRAINWORM
True sir, but I did need a broker, *ergo*.

WELLBRED
Well put off – no crafty knave, you'll say.

EDWARD
Tut, he has more of these shifts.

BRAINWORM
And yet where I have one, the broker has ten, sir.

[*Enter* CASH]

12–13 *hackney* plodding, from the gait of a hired horse

14 *shove-groat shilling* a coin used in a shuffleboard game called shove-groat

15 *reformados* officers left without command (owing to the 'reforming' or disband-
ing of their company) (OED)

22 *artificer* an artful or wily person; a trickster (OED); Edward picks up on the
sense of 'contriver, inventor, deviser', comparable to 'architect' (*sb.* 3).

27 *Houndsditch* a London street where disreputable old-clothes dealers known as
'brokers' sold their wares

33 *shifts* fraudulent or evasive devices, stratagems (OED); also, shirts, with both
meanings applicable as Brainworm replies punningly in the next line

CASH

Francis, Martin, ne'er a one to be found, now? What a   35
spite's this?

WELLBRED

How now, Thomas? Is my brother Kitely within?

CASH

No sir, my master went forth e'en now; but Master
Downright is within. Cob, what, Cob? Is he gone too?

WELLBRED

Whither went your master, Thomas, canst thou tell?   40

CASH

I know not, to Justice Clement's, I think, sir. Cob!   [*Exit*]

EDWARD

Justice Clement, what's he?

WELLBRED

Why, dost thou not know him? He is a City magistrate, a
justice here, an excellent good lawyer, and a great scholar;
but the only mad, merry, old fellow in Europe! I showed   45
him you, the other day.

EDWARD

Oh, is that he? I remember him now. Good faith, and he
has a very strange presence, methinks; it shows as if he
stood out of the rank from other men. I have heard many
of his jests i' university. They say, he will commit a man for   50
taking the wall of his horse.

WELLBRED

Aye, or wearing his cloak of one shoulder, or serving of
God: anything indeed, if it come in the way of his humour.

[CASH] *goes in and out calling*

CASH

Gaspar, Martin, Cob! 'Heart, where should they be, trow?

BOBADILL

Master Kitely's man, 'pray thee vouchsafe us the lighting of   55
this match.

35 *ne'er a one* not one

35–6 *What a spite's this?* i.e. Isn't that exasperating?

45 *only* most

51 *taking the wall* passing nearer the wall, where the road was cleaner – a privilege
   of social superiors, but not normally of their horses

55 *vouchsafe* to make a grant of something (OED)

CASH

Fire on your match, no time but now to vouchsafe? Francis,
Cob!   [*Exit*]

BOBADILL

Body of me! Here's the remainder of seven pound, since
yesterday was seven-night. 'Tis your right Trinidado! Did   60
you never take any, Master Stephen?

STEPHEN

No truly, sir; but I'll learn to take it now, since you commend it so.

BOBADILL

Sir, believe me (upon my relation), for what I tell you, the
world shall not reprove. I have been in the Indies (where   65
this herb grows), where neither myself, nor a dozen gentlemen more (of my knowledge) have received the taste of any
other nutriment in the world, for the space of one and
twenty weeks, but the fume of this simple only. Therefore,
it cannot be but 'tis most divine! Further, take it in the   70
nature, in the true kind so, it makes an antidote that, had
you taken the most deadly poisonous plant in all Italy, it
should expel it, and clarify you, with as much ease as I
speak. And, for your green wound, your Balsamum and
your St. John's wort are all mere gulleries, and trash to it, 75
especially your Trinidado; your Nicotian is good too. I

---

57 *Fire on* A version of 'fie on', meaning something like, 'to hell with', playing in
    either case on the topic of a lit match.

59–60 *Here's ... seven-night* i.e. This is all that's left of seven pounds of tobacco
    bought eight days ago

60 *Trinidado* tobacco of the highest quality from Trinidad

64–83 *Sir, believe me ... use of man* Bobadill's speech is (as Edward's reply sug-
    gests) a pastiche of the enthusiastic claims being made for tobacco at the time.

65 *reprove* disprove

65–9 *I ... only* Bobadill goes well beyond accounts of travellers who used tobacco
    in place of food (or to stave off hunger) for four or five days, as in Hakluyt,
    Principall Navigations ..., 1589, p. 541.

69 *simple* a single plant or herb employed for medical purposes

72 *Italy* Italy was popularly known in England as the poisoning capital of the world.

74 *green* fresh, unhealed, raw (OED)
    Balsamum an aromatic ointment used for soothing pain or healing wounds
    (OED)

75 *St. John's wort* medicinal plant used to arrest bleeding, close wounds, and soothe
    burns
    gulleries deceptions, tricks

76 *Nicotian* tobacco, from the name of Jacques Nicot, credited with introducing
    tobacco into France. Bobadill does not know that Nicotian is a generic term.

could say what I know of the virtue of it, for the expulsion
of rheums, raw humours, crudities, obstructions, with a
thousand of this kind; but I profess myself no quacksalver.
Only, thus much, by Hercules, I do hold it, and will affirm   80
it (before any prince in Europe) to be the most sovereign
and precious weed that ever the earth tendered to the use of
man.

EDWARD
This speech would ha' done decently in a tobacco-trader's
mouth!   85

[*Enter* CASH *and* COB]

CASH
At Justice Clement's, he is: in the middle of Coleman Street.

COB
Oh, oh!

BOBADILL
Where's the match I gave thee? Master Kitely's man?

CASH
Would his match, and he, and pipe, and all were at Santo
Domingo! I had forgot it.   [*Exit*]   90

COB
By God's me, I mar'l what pleasure or felicity they have in
taking this roguish tobacco! It's good for nothing but to
choke a man, and fill him full of smoke and embers: there
were four died out of one house, last week, with taking of
it, and two more the bell went for yesternight; one of them   95
(they say) will ne'er scape it: he voided a bushel of soot yesterday, upward and downward. By the stocks, an' there
were no wiser man than I, I'd have it present whipping,
man or woman, that should but deal with a tobacco-pipe;

---

78 *rheums* colds in the head or lungs; catarrhs
    crudities imperfectly 'concocted' (digested or 'cooked') humours (OED)
79 *quacksalver* an ignorant person who pretends to a knowledge of medicine or of
    wonderful remedies (OED)
89–90 *Santo Domingo* a West Indian island (or its capital), famous as a tobacco-
    growing region; see the note on Bobadill's name above, under Persons of the Play
91–101 *By God's me … rosaker* Cob's speech accurately reflects the other side in
    the tobacco debate, which culminated in King James's own 1604 tract *A
    Counterblaste to Tobacco.*
95 *bell went for* A bell was rung for the dead, or here, for those nearing death.
96–7 *voided … downward* i.e. vomited and defecated a bushel of tobacco ash
98 *present* immediate

why, it will stifle them all in the end, as many as use it; it's   100
little better than ratsbane, or rosaker.

BOBADILL beats [COB] with a cudgel

ALL
  Oh, good Captain, hold, hold.
BOBADILL
  You base cullion, you.

[Enter CASH, with the lighted match]

CASH
  Sir, here's your match; [<i>To</i> COB] come, thou must needs be
  talking, too, thou'rt well enough served.   105
COB
  Nay, he will not meddle with his match, I warrant you;
  well, it shall be a dear beating, an' I live.
BOBADILL
  Do you prate? Do you murmur?
EDWARD
  Nay, good Captain, will you regard the humour of a fool?
  [<i>To</i> COB] Away, knave.   110
WELLBRED
  Thomas, get him away.

[Exit CASH and COB]

BOBADILL
  A whoreson filthy slave, a dung-worm, an excrement! Body
  o' Caesar, but that I scorn to let forth so mean a spirit, I'd
  ha' stabbed him to the earth.
WELLBRED
  Marry, the law forbid, sir.   115
BOBADILL
  By Pharaoh's foot, I would have done it.
STEPHEN
  [<i>Aside</i>] Oh, he swears admirably! By Pharaoh's foot! Body
  o' Caesar! I shall never do it, sure, upon mine honour, and
  by St. George, no, I ha' not the right grace.

---

101 <i>ratsbane</i> rat-poison; specifically arsenic (OED)
     rosaker realgar, also called 'red arsenic'
103 <i>cullion</i> testicle; used as a term of contempt: a base, despicable, or vile fellow; a
     rascal (OED)
106 <i>meddle ... match</i> i.e. fight his equal, pick on someone his own size (Tilley
     M747); with a play on the match used to light the pipes

MATTHEW
  Master Stephen, will you any? By this air, the most divine 120
  tobacco that ever I drunk!
STEPHEN
  None, I thank you, sir.

                    [*Exit* BOBADILL *and* MATTHEW]

  Oh, this gentleman does it rarely too! But nothing like the
  other. By this air, as I am a gentleman: by – (*Practising to
  the post*)
BRAINWORM
  [*Aside*] Master, glance, glance! Master Wellbred!   125
STEPHEN
  As I have somewhat to be saved, I protest –
WELLBRED
  You are a fool; it needs no affidavit.
EDWARD
  Cousin, will you any tobacco?
STEPHEN
  Aye, sir! Upon my reputation –
EDWARD
  How now, cousin!   130
STEPHEN
  I protest, as I am a gentleman, but no soldier, indeed –
WELLBRED
  No, Master Stephen? As I remember, your name is entered
  in the Artillery Garden.
STEPHEN
  Aye, sir, that's true: cousin, may I swear, as I am a soldier,
  by that?   135
EDWARD
  Oh yes, that you may. It's all you have for your money.
STEPHEN
  Then, as I am a gentleman, and a soldier, it is divine
  tobacco!

121 *drunk* an affected but not unknown synonym for 'smoked'
124 s.d. *Practising to the post* rehearsing his swearing, his fencing, or both, with a
    pillar as his audience or opponent; recent studies suggest that theatres such as the
    Globe had support pillars near the front of the stage on either side.
125 *glance* Brainworm whispers to them to look at Stephen's ridiculous behaviour.
127 *affidavit* statement made on faith or oath (OED); Wellbred picks up on Stephen's
    'I protest' as a solemn vow
133 *Artillery Garden* training yard of the Honourable Artillery Company, a citizen
    militia founded in 1507; the company had become militarily obsolete before it
    was reorganized in 1610–11.

WELLBRED
  But soft, where's Master Matthew? Gone?
BRAINWORM
  No, sir, they went in here.   140
WELLBRED
  Oh, let's follow them: Master Matthew is gone to salute
  his mistress, in verse. We shall ha' the happiness to hear
  some of his poetry now. He never comes unfurnished.
  Brainworm?
STEPHEN
  Brainworm? Where? Is this Brainworm?   145
EDWARD
  Aye, cousin, no words of it, upon your gentility.
STEPHEN
  Not I, body of me, by this air, St. George, and the foot of
  Pharaoh!
WELLBRED
  Rare! Your cousin's discourse is simply drawn out with
  oaths.   150
EDWARD
  'Tis larded with 'em. A kind of French dressing, if you love
  it.

                                                         [*Exeunt*]

Act III, Scene iv

                    [*Enter*] KITELY [*and*] COB

KITELY
  Ha? How many are there, sayest thou?
COB
  Marry, sir, your brother, Master Wellbred –
KITELY
  Tut, beside him: what strangers are there, man?
COB
  Strangers? Let me see, one, two: mass, I know not well,
  there are so many.   5

---

139 *soft* i.e. wait a minute, be quiet
149–50 *drawn out with oaths* bulked up by adding filler, with a pun on 'oats', a
    homophone of 'oaths' in Elizabethan pronunciation
151 *French dressing* A pun on the noted French practices of elegant swearing and of
    'larding': inserting small strips of fat into meat before cooking. Jackson further
    suggests that this plays on Wellbred's preceding line, since a bird would be dis-
    embowelled – 'drawn out' – before it was larded.

KITELY
  How? So many?
COB
  Aye, there's some five, or six of them, at most.
KITELY
  [*Aside*] A swarm, a swarm,
  Spite of the devil, how they sting my head
  With forkèd stings, thus wide and large!
  [*He holds up fingers to indicate horns on his head*]
                                But, Cob,   10
  How long hast thou been coming hither, Cob?
COB
  A little while, sir.
KITELY
  Didst thou come running?
COB
  No, sir.
KITELY
  Nay, then I am familiar with thy haste!   15
  [*Aside*] Bane to my fortunes! What meant I to marry?
  I, that before was ranked in such content,
  My mind at rest too, in so soft a peace,
  Being free master of mine own free thoughts,
  And now become a slave? What? Never sigh,   20
  Be of good cheer, man: for thou art a cuckold,
  'Tis done, 'tis done! Nay, when such flowing store,
  Plenty itself, falls in my wife's lap,
  The *cornu-copiae* will be mine, I know. But, Cob,
  What entertainment had they? I am sure   25
  My sister, and my wife, would bid them welcome! Ha?
COB
  Like enough, sir, yet I heard not a word of it.

Act III, Scene iv This is III.vi in F.

  9–10 *sting ... forkèd stings* The swarming strangers, likened to insects or serpents,
     'sting' Kitely's head by infuriating him, by making him sprout horns (Kitely thus
     conflates 'stings' with insect antennae), and perhaps by making him imagine an
     invasion by the 'sting' or 'sharp-pointed organ' that symbolized the penis
     (Williams). See II.i.238n and III.ii.77n.
  16 *Bane* Poison; this and Kitely's complaints at II.i. 109–12, 208–10, and 225–7
     are clearly echoed by Shakespeare's jealous Othello (III.iii).
  22–3 *flowing ... lap* Kitely alludes to Zeus's sexual assault on Danae in the form of
     a shower of gold.
  24 *cornu-copiae* the horns of plenty, but such plenitude in his wife's lap means
     cuckold's horns for him
  25 *entertainment* manner of reception (OED)

KITELY

No: their lips were sealed with kisses, and the voice
Drowned in a flood of joy, at their arrival,
Had lost her motion, state, and faculty.   30
Cob, which of them was't, that first kissed my wife?
My sister, I should say; my wife, alas,
I fear not her: ha? Who was it, say'st thou?

COB

By my troth, sir, will you have the truth of it?

KITELY

Oh aye, good Cob: I pray thee, heartily.   35

COB

Then, I am a vagabond, and fitter for Bridewell than your
worship's company, if I saw anybody to be kissed, unless
they would have kissed the post in the middle of the warehouse; for there I left them all, at their tobacco, with a pox.

KITELY

How? Were they not gone in, then, ere thou cam'st?   40

COB

Oh, no, sir.

KITELY

Spite of the devil! What do I stay here, then? Cob, follow
me.   [Exit]

COB

Nay, soft and fair, I have eggs on the spit: I cannot go yet,
sir. Now am I for some five and fifty reasons hammering,   45
hammering revenge; oh, for three or four gallons of vinegar, to sharpen my wits. Revenge; vinegar revenge; vinegar
and mustard revenge; nay, an' he had not lyen in my house,
'twould never have grieved me, but being my guest, one
that I'll be sworn my wife has lent him her smock off her   50
back, while his one shirt has been at washing; pawned her
neckerchers for clean bands for him; sold almost all my

---

30 *motion* inward prompting or impulse (OED *sv* 9.a), or ability to produce sound
    (cf. move *v.* 4)
    state proper or normal condition (OED)
    faculty physical capability or function (OED)
36 *Bridewell* a prison and workhouse for vagabonds and the poor; for the meaning
    of Cob's construction here, see III.ii.47n above.
38 *kissed the post* Cob plays on a proverbial expression for being left out of a party
    (Tilley P494).
39 *with a pox* i.e. wishing a plague on them (cf. Tilley M1003)
44 *Nay ... spit* i.e. No, take it easy, I have other business in hand (Tilley S601, E86);
    the expression refers to the tending of roasting eggs.
52 *bands* collars or ruffs

platters, to buy him tobacco; and he to turn monster of
ingratitude, and strike his lawful host! Well, I hope to raise
up an host of fury for't: here comes Justice Clement.   55

        [*Enter*] CLEMENT, KNOWELL [*and*] FORMAL

CLEMENT
What, 's Master Kitely gone? Roger?
FORMAL
Aye, sir.
CLEMENT
'Heart of me! What made him leave us so abruptly? How
now, sirrah? What make you here? What would you have,
ha?   60
COB
An't please your worship, I am a poor neighbour of your
worship's –
CLEMENT
A poor neighbour of mine? Why, speak, poor neighbour.
COB
I dwell, sir, at the sign of the Water-tankard, hard by the
Green Lattice; I have paid scot and lot there, any time this   65
eighteen years.
CLEMENT
To the Green Lattice?
COB
No, sir, to the parish; marry, I have seldom scaped scot-
free, at the Lattice.
CLEMENT
Oh, well! What business has my poor neighbour with me?   70
COB
An't like your worship, I am come to crave the peace of
your worship.
CLEMENT
Of me, knave? Peace of me, knave? Did I e'er hurt thee? Or
threaten thee? Or wrong thee? Ha?

---

54 *host* an army, often of heavenly forces
55 s.d. *Enter* CLEMENT ... III.vii begins here in F.
64 *at the sign of the Water-tankard* Cob identifies his house by the formula usually
    used for an inn.
65 *Green Lattice* A window of lattice-work (usually painted red), or a pattern on
    the shutter or wall imitating this, was formerly a common mark of an alehouse
    or inn (OED).
    scot and lot a tax levied by a municipal corporation (OED; cf. Tilley S159)
71 *crave the peace* Cob seeks a warrant to restrain Bobadill from violence against
    him.

COB

No, sir, but your worship's warrant, for one that has   75
wronged me, sir: his arms are at too much liberty, I would
fain have them bound to a treaty of peace, an' my credit
could compass it with your worship.

CLEMENT

Thou goest far enough about for't, I'm sure.

KNOWELL

Why, dost thou go in danger of thy life for him, friend?   80

COB

No sir; but I go in danger of my death, every hour, by his
means: an' I die within a twelve-month and a day, I may
swear, by the law of the land, that he killed me.

CLEMENT

How? How knave? Swear he killed thee? And by the law?
What pretence? What colour hast thou for that?   85

COB

Marry, an't please your worship, both black and blue:
colour enough, I warrant you. I have it here, to show your
worship.

CLEMENT

What is he that gave you this, sirrah?

COB

A gentleman, and a soldier, he says he is, o' the City here.   90

CLEMENT

A soldier o' the City? What call you him?

COB

Captain Bobadill.

CLEMENT

Bobadill? And why did he bob and beat you, sirrah? How
began the quarrel betwixt you: ha? Speak truly, knave, I
advise you.   95

COB

Marry, indeed, an' please your worship, only because I

---

78 *compass it* i.e. bring it about, accomplish it. Clement picks up on another meaning, 'go round, make a circuit'.

82-3 *an' I die ... me* A murder indictment could be brought within a year and a
day of the crime, so if Cob dies of his wounds during this period, Bobadill could
face a capital charge.

85 *What pretence ... that?* What could be the grounds or argument for such a
claim?

93 *bob* a blow with the fist (OED); Clement plays on Bobadill's name.

spake against their vagrant tobacco, as I came by 'em, when
they were taking on't; for nothing else.

CLEMENT
Ha? You speak against tobacco? Formal, his name.

FORMAL
What's your name, sirrah?   100

COB
Oliver, sir, Oliver Cob, sir.

CLEMENT
Tell Oliver Cob, he shall go to the jail, Formal.

FORMAL
Oliver Cob, my master, Justice Clement, says, you shall go
to the jail.

COB
Oh, I beseech your worship, for God's sake, dear Master   105
Justice.

CLEMENT
Nay, God's precious: an' such drunkards, and tankards, as
you are, come to dispute of tobacco once – I have done!
Away with him.

COB
Oh, good Master Justice, sweet old gentleman.   110

KNOWELL
Sweet Oliver, would I could do thee any good: Justice
Clement, let me entreat you, sir.

CLEMENT
What? A threadbare rascal! A beggar! A slave that never
drunk out of better than piss-pot metal in his life! And he
to deprave and abuse the virtue of an herb so generally   115
received in the courts of princes, the chambers of nobles,
the bowers of sweet ladies, the cabins of soldiers! Roger,
away with him, by God's precious – I say, go to.

---

97 *vagrant* Vagrancy was a charge against those (such as actors) who travelled without home or livelihood; figuratively, base, good-for-nothing, thievish; perhaps
   with a play on the sense of 'wandering' (with reference to smoke).

107 *tankards* i.e. tankard-bearers, water carriers (see I.ii.95); a tankard was also a
    drinking-vessel such as the drunkards would use.

111 *Sweet Oliver* An epithet which appears repeatedly, playing on a catch-phrase
    from a popular song of the period, with an echo in Shakespeare's *As You Like
    It*, a possible source in Ariosto's *Orlando Furioso*, and a comically inappropri-
    ate connotation of high living; cf. Tilley O40.

114 *piss-pot metal* pewter, used for chamber-pots

117 *cabins* See I.iv.33n.

COB

Dear Master Justice: let me be beaten again, I have deserved
it; but not the prison, I beseech you.   120

KNOWELL

Alas, poor Oliver!

CLEMENT

Roger, make him a warrant – he shall not go – I but fear
the knave.

FORMAL

Do not stink, sweet Oliver, you shall not go, my master will
give you a warrant.   125

COB

Oh, the Lord maintain his worship, his worthy worship.

CLEMENT

Away, dispatch him.

[*Exeunt* FORMAL *and* COB]

How now, Master Knowell! In dumps? In dumps? Come,
this becomes not.

KNOWELL

Sir, would I could not feel my cares –   130

CLEMENT

Your cares are nothing! They are like my cap, soon put on,
and as soon put off. What? Your son is old enough to
govern himself: let him run his course, it's the only way to
make him a staid man. If he were an unthrift, a ruffian, a
drunkard, or a licentious liver, then you had reason: you   135
had reason to take care; but, being none of these, mirth's
my witness, an' I had twice so many cares as you have, I'd
drown them all in a cup of sack. Come, come, let's try it; I
muse your parcel of a soldier returns not all this while.

[*Exeunt*]

---

122 *fear* frighten

124 *Do not stink, sweet Oliver* probably, 'don't shit yourself', i.e. don't be afraid;
hence perhaps Cob's reference at IV.ii.23 to the 'filthy fear' this threat of jail pro-
voked, with potential for some bathroom-humour stage-business

128 *In dumps* Despondent

134 *staid* dignified, with a paradoxical play on 'stayed', restrained, the opposite of
being allowed to run his course (on which expression, see I.i.205 above, and
Tilley Y48)

138 *sack* A general name for a class of white wines formerly imported from Spain
and the Canaries (OED); the word derives from French *vin sec*, 'dry wine',
although it came to be used for sweet wines as well, especially sherry.

139 *I muse your parcel* i.e. I am perplexed that your little piece (used contemptuously)

Act IV, Scene i

[Enter] DOWNRIGHT *[and]* DAME KITELY

DOWNRIGHT
Well, sister, I tell you true; and you'll find it so, in the end.
DAME KITELY
Alas, brother, what would you have me to do? I cannot
help it: you see, my brother brings 'em in here, they are his
friends.
DOWNRIGHT
His friends? His fiends. 'Slud, they do nothing but haunt   5
him, up and down, like a sort of unlucky sprites, and tempt
him to all manner of villainy that can be thought of. Well,
by this light, a little thing would make me play the devil
with some of 'em; an't were not more for your husband's
sake than anything else, I'd make the house too hot for the   10
best on 'em: they should say, and swear, hell were broken
loose ere they went hence. But, by God's will, 'tis nobody's
fault but yours: for, an' you had done as you might have
done, they should have been parboiled, and baked too,
every mother's son, ere they should ha' come in, e'er a one   15
of 'em.
DAME KITELY
God's my life! Did you ever hear the like? What a strange
man is this! Could I keep out all them, think you? I should
put myself against half a dozen men, should I? Good faith,
you'd mad the patient'st body in the world, to hear you talk 20
so, without any sense or reason!

[Enter] MISTRESS BRIDGET, MASTER MATTHEW, *[and]*
BOBADILL, *[followed by]* WELLBRED, STEPHEN,
EDWARD *[and]* BRAINWORM

---

5 *'Slud* Apparently a variant of *'Sblood* (i.e. 'God's blood') (OED).
6 *sprites* spirits
8 *a little thing would* it would not take much to (Dent T141.11)
14 *parboiled* thoroughly boiled (now an obsolete sense); Downright's speech is
  again peppered with proverbs (Dent-S H356.1, Tilley H403, M1202), adding up
  to little more than, 'I would have liked to beat the hell out of all of them'.
21 s.d. *Enter MISTRESS BRIDGET* ... IV.ii begins here in F; Edward and Wellbred
  observe the proceedings (including Downright's increasing agitation) and offer
  their asides from some distance, presumably downstage.

BRIDGET
Servant, in troth, you are too prodigal
Of your wit's treasure, thus to pour it forth
Upon so mean a subject as my worth.
MATTHEW
You say well, mistress; and I mean as well.   25
DOWNRIGHT
Hoy-day, here is stuff!
WELLBRED
Oh, now stand close; pray heaven she can get him to read;
he should do it of his own natural impudency.
BRIDGET
Servant, what is this same, I pray you?
MATTHEW
Marry, an elegy, an elegy, an odd toy –   30
DOWNRIGHT
To mock an ape withal. Oh, I could sew up his mouth now.
DAME KITELY
Sister, I pray you let's hear it.
DOWNRIGHT
Are you rhyme-given, too?
MATTHEW
Mistress, I'll read it, if you please.
BRIDGET
Pray you do, servant.   35
DOWNRIGHT
Oh, here's no foppery! Death, I can endure the stocks
better.   [Exit]
EDWARD
What ails thy brother? Can he not hold his water at read-
ing of a ballad?

---

22 *Servant* a professed admirer; one who is devoted to the service of a lady (OED)
25 *mistress* the corresponding term to 'servant': the lady being served and courted
26 *Hoy-day* a form of 'Hey-dey', an exclamation denoting surprise, wonder, etc.
   (OED)
   stuff worthless nonsense
27 *close* secretly, covertly (OED)
30 *odd toy* casual, trifling piece of writing
30–1 *toy … ape* a trick to deceive (or make sport of) a fool (Tilley T456)
33 *rhyme-given* i.e. given to rhyme, a devotee of poetry
36 *here's no foppery* i.e. here's no foolishness (meant sarcastically)
   Death an oath, meaning 'By God's death'
38 *hold his water* refrain from urinating

WELLBRED
Oh, no: a rhyme to him is worse than cheese or a bagpipe.   40
But, mark, you lose the protestation.
MATTHEW
Faith, I did it in an humour: I know not how it is; but,
please you come near, sir. This gentleman has judgement,
he knows how to censure of a – pray you sir, you can judge.
STEPHEN
Not I, sir: upon my reputation, and by the foot of Pharaoh.   45
WELLBRED
Oh, chide your cousin for swearing.
EDWARD
Not I, so long as he does not forswear himself.
BOBADILL
Master Matthew, you abuse the expectation of your dear
mistress, and her fair sister: fie, while you live, avoid this
prolixity.   50
MATTHEW
I shall, sir: well, *Incipere dulce.*
EDWARD
How! *Insipere dulce*? A sweet thing to be a fool, indeed.
WELLBRED
What, do you take *Incipere* in that sense?
EDWARD
You do not? You? This was your villainy, to gull him with
a *mot.*   55

---

40 *cheese ... bagpipe* supposed diuretics on susceptible people; Shakespeare's
Shylock mentions people who, 'when the bagpipe sings i' th' nose / Cannot contain their urine' (*Merchant of Venice* IV.i.49–50).
41 *mark ... protestation* i.e. listen, you're missing Matthew's claims and excuses for
his poetry
42 *how it is* i.e. whether it is good
47 *forswear himself* break his vow – impossible if he lacks judgement or reputation
51 *Incipere dulce* To begin is sweet
52 *Insipere ... indeed* Edward pretends to hear the potential homonym *insipere*, 'to
be a fool'; cf. Tilley K188: 'knowing nothing is the sweetest life'.
55 *mot* motto; the sense of 'witty saying' also seems present, although OED does
not find this meaning until 1631

WELLBRED

Oh, the benchers' phrase: *pauca verba, pauca verba.*

MATTHEW

'*Rare creature, let me speak without offence,*
Would God my rude words had the influence,
To rule thy thoughts, as thy fair looks do mine,
Then should'st thou be his prisoner, who is thine.'   60

EDWARD

This is in *Hero and Leander*?

WELLBRED

Oh, ay! Peace, we shall have more of this.

MATTHEW

'*Be not unkind and fair, misshapen stuff*
Is of behaviour boisterous, and rough.'

WELLBRED

How like you that, sir?   65

STEPHEN *answers with shaking his head*

EDWARD

'Slight, he shakes his head like a bottle, to feel an' there be
any brain in it!

MATTHEW

But observe the catastrophe, now:
'*And I in duty will exceed all other,*
As you in beauty do excel love's mother.'   70

EDWARD

Well, I'll have him free of the wit-brokers, for he utters
nothing but stol'n remnants.

WELLBRED

Oh, forgive it him.

---

56 *benchers'* a bencher might be (1) one who frequents the benches of a tavern; (2)
   a judge; or (3) a senior member of the Inns of Court (OED, citing this line under
   (1)). H&S assumes that Wellbred's 'benchers' are ale-house loungers. See next n.
   pauca verba 'few words' (Latin); the English phrase appeared in several
   proverbs, such as 'few words are best' (Tilley W798), and the Latin catch-phrase
   may have been associated with some of the 'benchers' above. Justice Overdo in
   Jonson's *Bartholomew Fair* uses this and similar phrases to recommend silence.
   For tavern 'benchers', the phrase implied 'Drink more, and talk less' (H&S).
61 *Hero and Leander* a famous narrative poem by Christopher Marlowe
   (1564–93), published posthumously in 1598, about a pair of ill-fated lovers;
   Matthew slightly misquotes the lines.
68 *catastrophe* the change or revolution which produces the conclusion or final
   event of a dramatic piece; the dénouement (OED)
71 *free of the wit-brokers* i.e. an official member of the (imaginary) London guild
   of second-hand wit dealers

EDWARD
A filching rogue? Hang him. And from the dead? It's worse
than sacrilege.   75
WELLBRED
Sister, what ha' you here? Verses? Pray you, let's see. Who
made these verses? They are excellent good!
MATTHEW
Oh, Master Wellbred, 'tis your disposition to say so sir.
They were good i' the morning, I made 'em, *extempore*, this
morning.   80
WELLBRED
How? *Extempore*?
MATTHEW
I would I might be hanged else; ask Captain Bobadill. He
saw me write them, at the – (pox on it) the Star, yonder.
BRAINWORM
Can he find, in his heart, to curse the stars so?
EDWARD
Faith, his are even with him: they ha' cursed him enough   85
already.
STEPHEN
Cousin, how do you like this gentleman's verses?
EDWARD
Oh, admirable! The best that ever I heard, coz!
STEPHEN
Body o' Caesar! They are admirable! The best that ever I
heard, as I am a soldier.   90

[*Enter* DOWNRIGHT]

DOWNRIGHT
I am vexed, I can hold ne'er a bone of me still! Heart! I
think they mean to build and breed here!
WELLBRED
Sister, you have a simple servant here, that crowns your

---

79 *good i' the morning* Matthew defends his poetry as if he were selling perishable
food.

extempore composed extemporaneously, without preparation or revision

83 *Star* a tavern

85 *his are ... enough* i.e. his stars have earned his curse, since his birth and destiny
(commonly called, via astrology, his 'stars') have made him such a pathetic figure

89–90 *Body ... soldier* Apparently set as verse in F; though the lines approximate
iambic pentameter, there is no reason to suppose Stephen has risen uncharacter-
istically to verse here, unless perhaps inspired by Matthew's recitation.

92 *build and breed* i.e. set up house, but in terms suggesting gulls

beauty with such *encomions*, and devices; you may see
what it is to be the mistress of a wit that can make your per-   95
fections so transparent that every blear eye may look
through them, and see him drowned over head and ears, in
the deep well of desire. Sister Kitely, I marvel you get you
not a servant that can rhyme and do tricks, too.

DOWNRIGHT

Oh, monster! Impudence itself! Tricks?   100

DAME KITELY

Tricks, brother? What tricks?

BRIDGET

Nay, speak, I pray you, what tricks?

DAME KITELY

Aye, never spare anybody here; but say, what tricks?

BRIDGET

Passion of my heart! Do tricks?

WELLBRED

'Slight, here's a trick vied, and revied! Why, you monkeys,   105
you! What a caterwauling do you keep? Has he not given
you rhymes, and verses, and tricks?

DOWNRIGHT

Oh, the fiend!

WELLBRED

Nay, you, lamp of virginity, that take it in snuff so! Come
and cherish this tame 'poetical fury' in your servant, you'll   110
be begged else, shortly, for a concealment: go to, reward his

---

94 *encomions* the Greek form of 'encomiums', formal or high-flown expressions of
   praise (OED)

96 *blear* dim

99 *do tricks* i.e. use clever poetic devices

100 *Tricks* Downright takes the sense 'sexual acts' (Williams); a pun was current on
   'merry tricks' and the Latin *meretrix*, prostitute.

105 *vied, and revied* card-playing terminology: bid and rebid
    monkeys Monkeys were noted for mimicry.

109 *lamp of virginity* symbolic of female virtue; cf. Dent L44.11
    take it in snuff so i.e. take so much offence (cf. Tilley S598), with punning ref-
    erence to the burned portion of the wick of a lamp

110 *'poetical fury'* a conventional phrase, from the Latin *furor poeticus*, for artistic
    inspiration

111 *concealment* Wellbred makes a complicated topical joke, having to do with con-
    troversial rewards claimed from Queen Elizabeth for those discovering property
    that was taken from the monasteries under Henry VIII but never given to the
    crown. So Matthew is (dishonestly, like many concealment-hunters) laying claim
    to Marlowe's poetic property, and his sovereign mistress must give him money
    for the portion passed on to her.

muse. You cannot give him less than a shilling, in conscience, for the book he had it out of cost him a teston, at
least. How now, gallants? Master Matthew? Captain?
What? All sons of silence? No spirit?   115

DOWNRIGHT
Come, you might practice your ruffian-tricks somewhere
else, and not here, I wuss: this is no tavern, nor drinking-
school, to vent your exploits in.

WELLBRED
How now! Whose cow has calved?

DOWNRIGHT
Marry, that has mine, sir. Nay, boy, never look askance at   120
me for the matter; I'll tell you of it, aye, sir, you, and your
companions, mend yourselves, when I ha' done.

WELLBRED
My companions?

DOWNRIGHT
Yes sir, your companions, so I say, I am not afraid of you,
nor them neither: your hang-bys here. You must have your   125
poets, and your potlings, your *soldados*, and *foolados*, to
follow you up and down the City, and here they must come
to domineer, and swagger. [*To* MATTHEW *and* BOBADILL]
Sirrah, you, ballad-singer, and slops, your fellow there, get
you out: get you home; or, by this steel, I'll cut off your   130
ears, and that presently.

WELLBRED
'Slight, stay, let's see what he dare do: cut off his ears? Cut

---

113 *teston* a name for the sixpenny piece (OED)

117 *I wuss* certainly

119 *Whose ... calved?* What's the matter? (Tilley C756); premature calving – 'casting' – is implied. Cf. *Gammer Gurton's Needle* (1566), IV.i.22: 'Hath your
brown cow cast her calf?'

120–1 *Marry ... of it* i.e. By Mary, my cow has. Oh no, you little nobody, don't give
me that look, I'm going to attack you (physically or verbally) for your behaviour

126 *potlings* votaries of the pot, tipplers (OED, citing only this line); probably also a
play on 'poetlings' (though OED does not find this word until 1772).
soldados, and foolados soldiers (Spanish) and fools (*faux* Spanish)

129 *slops* A synecdoche for Bobadill, who sports these 'wide baggy breeches ... commonly worn in the sixteenth and early seventeenth centuries' (OED).

132–3 *Cut a whetstone* i.e. You'll do no such thing. Accius Naevius did cut a whetstone with a razor in Roman myth, but George Chapman's Bussy D'Ambois
alludes to the legend to the same effect as Wellbred: 'Cut my throat? Cut a whetstone; good Accius Naevius, do as much with your tongue as he did with a razor;
cut my throat?' (1606; sig. B2v; cited H&S).

a whetstone. You are an ass, do you see? Touch any man
here, and by this hand, I'll run my rapier to the hilts in you.

DOWNRIGHT

Yea, that would I fain see, boy.   135

*They all draw, and they of the house make out to part
them*

DAME KITELY

Oh Jesu! Murder! Thomas, Gaspar!

[*Enter* CASH]

BRIDGET

Help, help, Thomas.

EDWARD

Gentlemen, forbear, I pray you.

BOBADILL

Well, sirrah, you, Holofernes: by my hand, I will pink your
flesh full of holes with my rapier for this; I will, by this good   140
heaven.

They offer to fight again, and are parted

Nay, let him come, let him come, gentlemen, by the body of
St. George, I'll not kill him.

CASH

Hold, hold, good gentlemen.

DOWNRIGHT

You whoreson, bragging coistril.   145

[*Enter*] KITELY

KITELY

Why, how now? What's the matter? What's the stir here?
Whence springs the quarrel? Thomas! Where is he?
Put up your weapons, and put off this rage.
My wife and sister, they are cause of this –
What, Thomas? Where is this knave?   150

---

139 *Holofernes* (Biblical) Nebuchadnezzar's avenging general, murdered by Judith
with his own sword as he lay dead drunk. He was a stock tyrant of the stage,
and there may have been a pun on 'hollow furnace' suited to the accusation that
Downright is full of heated but empty threats.
    pink pierce, prick, or stab (OED)

141 s.d. *offer* attempt

145 *coistril* knave, base fellow (OED); the word originally denoted the groom of a
knight's horse

145 s.d. *Enter* KITELY IV.iii begins here in F.

CASH
  Here, sir.
WELLBRED
  Come, let's go: this is one of my brother's ancient humours,
  this.
STEPHEN
  I am glad nobody was hurt by his ancient humour.

> [*Exeunt* WELLBRED, STEPHEN, EDWARD, MATTHEW,
>   BOBADILL *and* BRAINWORM]

KITELY
  Why, how now, brother, who enforced this brawl?   155
DOWNRIGHT
  A sort of lewd rakehells, that care neither for God, nor the
  devil! And they must come here to read ballads, and
  roguery, and trash! I'll mar the knot of 'em ere I sleep, per-
  haps; especially Bob, there: he that's all manner of shapes!
  And 'Songs and Sonnets', his fellow.   160
BRIDGET
  Brother, indeed, you are too violent,
  Too sudden, in your humour; and you know
  My brother Wellbred's temper will not bear
  Any reproof, chiefly in such a presence,
  Where every slight disgrace he should receive   165
  Might wound him in opinion and respect.
DOWNRIGHT
  Respect? What talk you of respect 'mong such,
  As ha' nor spark of manhood, nor good manners?
  'Sdeynes, I am ashamed to hear you! Respect?   [*Exit*]
BRIDGET
  Yes, there was one a civil gentleman,   170
  And very worthily demeaned himself!

---

154 *ancient* long-established. Stephen does not find the humour's durability com-
     forting.
156 *rakehells* Shortened in modern usage to 'rake', the longer form had wider con-
     notations of 'thorough scoundrel or rascal; utterly immoral or dissolute person'
     (OED).
158 *mar* inflict destructive bodily harm upon (OED)
159 *all ... shapes* Downright is probably again referring to Bobadill's voluminous
     trousers.
160 *'Songs and Sonnets'* This title of Richard Tottel's popular verse anthology (1557)
     was commonly applied to such collections, which is all the complete works of
     Matthew amount to.
171 *demeaned* behaved, maintained his demeanour

KITELY

Oh, that was some love of yours, sister!

BRIDGET

A love of mine? I would it were no worse, brother!
You'd pay my portion sooner than you think for.

DAME KITELY

Indeed, he seemed to be a gentleman of an exceeding fair   175
disposition, and of very excellent good parts!

[Exeunt DAME KITELY *and* BRIDGET]

KITELY

Her love, by heaven! My wife's minion!
Fair disposition? Excellent good parts?
Death, these phrases are intolerable!
Good parts? How should she know his parts?   180
His parts? Well, well, well, well, well, well!
It is too plain, too clear. Thomas, come hither.
What, are they gone?

CASH   Aye, sir, they went in.

My mistress, and your sister –

KITELY

Are any of the gallants within?   185

CASH

No, sir, they are all gone.

KITELY

Art thou sure of it?

CASH

I can assure you, sir.

KITELY

What gentleman was that they praised so, Thomas?

CASH

One, they call him Master Knowell, a handsome young   190
gentleman, sir.

KITELY

Aye, I thought so: my mind gave me as much.
I'll die but they have hid him i' the house,
Somewhere; I'll go and search. Go with me, Thomas.
Be true to me, and thou shalt find me a master.   195

[Exeunt]

---

174 *portion* dowry, the bride's 'gift' to her husband

177 *minion* darling, lover

180 *parts* Dame Kitely meant 'personal qualities', but Kitely thinks of 'privy parts',
     or genitals. See III.ii.76n.

Act IV, Scene ii

[*Enter*] COB

COB
[*Knocking*] What, Tib! Tib, I say!
TIB
[*Within*] How now, what cuckold is that knocks so hard?

[TIB *opens the door and enters*]

Oh, husband, is't you? What's the news?
COB
Nay, you have stunned me, i' faith! You ha' giv'n me a
knock o' the forehead will stick by me! Cuckold? 'Slid,   5
cuckold?
TIB
Away, you fool, did I know it was you, that knocked?
Come, come, you may call me as bad, when you list.
COB
May I? Tib, you are a whore.
TIB
You lie in your throat, husband.   10
COB
How, the lie? And in my throat too? Do you long to be
stabbed, ha?
TIB
Why, you are no soldier, I hope?
COB
Oh, must you be stabbed by a soldier? Mass, that's true!
When was Bobadill here? Your captain? That rogue, that   15
foist, that fencing Burgullian? I'll tickle him, i' faith.

Act IV, Scene ii This is IV.iv in F.

  8 *list* desire, choose

10 *lie ... throat* The 'lie in the throat' was the most brazen, outrageous lie; accus-
    ing a soldier of this was provoking a fight to the death. See II.ii.4–5n.

14 *stabbed* Cob responds to the sense of 'penetrated sexually'.

16 *foist* cheat, rogue; pick-pocket (OED)
    Burgullian a form of Burgonian (or Burgundian); it refers to a notorious
    swordster, John Barrose, who was hanged for the murder of a City officer who
    had arrested him for debt; Barrose had previously challenged all the fencers in
    England (H&S).
    tickle ironically, to beat, chastise (OED)

TIB

Why, what's the matter? Trow!

COB

Oh, he has basted me, rarely, sumptuously! But I have it
here in black and white, [*Shows his warrant*] for his black
and blue, shall pay him. Oh, the Justice! The honestest old   20
brave Trojan in London! I do honour the very flea of his
dog. A plague on him though, he put me once in a villainous filthy fear; marry, it vanished away, like the smoke of
tobacco; but I was smoked soundly first. I thank the devil,
and his good angel, my guest. Well, wife, or Tib (which you   25
will), get you in, and lock the door, I charge you, let
nobody in to you; wife, nobody in to you: those are my
words. Not Captain Bob himself, nor the fiend in his likeness; you are a woman; you have flesh and blood enough in
you to be tempted: therefore, keep the door shut upon all   30
comers.

TIB

I warrant you, there shall nobody enter here, without my
consent.

COB

Nor with your consent, sweet Tib, and so I leave you.

TIB

It's more than you know, whether you leave me so.   35

COB

How?

TIB

Why, sweet.

COB

Tut, sweet, or sour, thou art a flower,
Keep close thy door, I ask no more.

[*Exit* COB *and* TIB, *separately*]

17 *Trow!* An exclamation without specific meaning.

18 *basted* beat soundly, thrashed (OED)

21 *Trojan* a brave or plucky fellow (OED); the English prided themselves on their
supposed descent from ancient Trojans

24 *smoked* made to suffer (see III.ii.193n, and Dent S576.11: 'vanish in smoke')

25 *his good angel, my guest* Cob depicts Bobadill as the devil's emissary.
wife, or Tib (which you will) i.e. wife, or the loose woman your name implies,
whichever you choose to be

29–31 *you have ... comers* Here as elsewhere, sexual innuendo derives from an
association between Tib's house and her body.

35 *It's more ... leave me so.* Playing off her husband's formulaic parting words, Tib
(who enjoys teasing him) says that he should not feel so sure he is leaving her in
a state of sweetness.

Act IV, Scene iii

[Enter] EDWARD, WELLBRED, STEPHEN *[and]*
BRAINWORM *[still disguised]*

EDWARD
Well, Brainworm, perform this business happily, and thou
makest a purchase of my love forever.
WELLBRED
I' faith, now let thy spirits use their best faculties. But, at
any hand, remember the message to my brother: for there's
no other means to start him.   5
BRAINWORM
I warrant you, sir, fear nothing: I have a nimble soul has
waked all forces of my fancy, by this time, and put 'em in
true motion. What you have possessed me withal, I'll dis-
charge it amply, sir. Make it no question.
WELLBRED
Forth, and prosper, Brainworm.   10

[Exit BRAINWORM*]*

Faith, Ned, how dost thou approve of my abilities in this
device?
EDWARD
Troth, well, howsoever; but it will come excellent, if it take.
WELLBRED
Take, man? Why, it cannot choose but take, if the circum-
stances miscarry not; but, tell me, ingenuously, dost thou   15
affect my sister Bridget, as thou pretend'st?
EDWARD
Friend, am I worth belief?
WELLBRED
Come, do not protest. In faith, she is a maid of good orna-

Act IV, Scene iii This is IV.v in F.

   1–2 *Well ... forever* Set as verse in F, breaking after 'happily'; but the second line
     is more anapestic than iambic, the rest of the scene is clearly prose, and Edward
     is not one of the characters who tends to speak in verse.

   5 *start* to force (an animal, especially a hare) to leave its lair (OED)

   8 *possessed me withal* i.e. instructed me in

 15–16 *ingenuously ... pretend'st?* i.e. honestly, do you love my sister Bridget as you
     claim to?

 18–19 *of good ornament* possessing desirable qualities, such as beauty, grace, or
     honour (OED 2b)

ment, and much modesty; and, except I conceived very
worthily of her, thou shouldest not have her.   20

EDWARD

Nay, that I am afraid will be a question yet, whether I shall
have her, or no.

WELLBRED

'Slid, thou shalt have her: by this light, thou shalt.

EDWARD

Nay, do not swear.

WELLBRED

By this hand, thou shalt have her: I'll go fetch her, pres-   25
ently. 'Point but where to meet, and as I am an honest man,
I'll bring her.

EDWARD

Hold, hold, be temperate.

WELLBRED

Why, by – what shall I swear by? Thou shalt have her, as I
am –   30

EDWARD

'Pray thee, be at peace, I am satisfied; and do believe thou
wilt omit no offered occasion to make my desires complete.

WELLBRED

Thou shalt see, and know, I will not.

[Exeunt]

Act IV, Scene iv

[Enter] FORMAL *[and]* KNOWELL

FORMAL

Was your man a soldier, sir?

KNOWELL

Aye, a knave, I took him begging o' the way,
This morning, as I came over Moorfields!

[Enter BRAINWORM, *still disguised]*

19–20 *except … have her* i.e. unless I thought very well of her, I would not allow
you to marry her

26 *'Point* Appoint, designate

Act IV, Scene iv This is IV.vi in F.

2 *took* overtook

3 *Moorfields* reclaimed marshlands north of the City, site of numerous activities
including military practice, duelling, and begging

Oh, here he is! You've made fair speed, believe me:
Where, i' the name of sloth, could you be thus –   5
BRAINWORM
Marry, peace be my comfort, where I thought I should have
had little comfort of your worship's service.
KNOWELL
How so?
BRAINWORM
Oh, sir! Your coming to the City, your entertainment of
me, and your sending me to watch – indeed, all the circum-   10
stances either of your charge, or my employment – are as
open to your son as to yourself!
KNOWELL
How should that be! Unless that villain, Brainworm,
Have told him of the letter, and discovered
All that I strictly charged him to conceal? 'Tis so!   15
BRAINWORM
I am partly o' the faith 'tis so indeed.
KNOWELL
But, how should he know thee to be my man?
BRAINWORM
Nay, sir, I cannot tell; unless it be by the black art! Is not
your son a scholar, sir?
KNOWELL
Yes, but I hope his soul is not allied   20
Unto such hellish practice: if it were,
I had just cause to weep my part in him,
And curse the time of his creation.
But, where didst thou find them, Fitzsword?
BRAINWORM
You should rather ask, where they found me, sir, for I'll be   25
sworn I was going along in the street, thinking nothing,
when (of a sudden) a voice calls, 'Master Knowell's man';
another cries, 'Soldier'; and thus, half a dozen of 'em, till
they had called me within a house where I no sooner came

---

6 *peace be my comfort* i.e. I comfort myself with the idea that at least death is
   peaceful
6–7 *where … service* i.e. I have been where I thought I would be made very
   uncomfortable because I was working for you; or, where I feared I would not
   survive to continue the pleasure of working for you
9 *entertainment* employment
12 *open* patent, evident, plain (OED)
18–19 *black … scholar* Well-known plays such as Marlowe's *Doctor Faustus* and
   Greene's *Friar Bacon and Friar Bungay* explore the association between scholarship and black magic.

but they seemed men, and out flew all their rapiers at my   30
bosom, with some three- or four-score oaths to accompany
'em, and all to tell me I was but a dead man, if I did not
confess where you were, and how I was employed, and
about what; which, when they could not get out of me (as
I protest, they must ha' dissected and made an anatomy o'   35
me first, and so I told 'em) they locked me up into a room
i' the top of a high house, whence, by great miracle (having
a light heart) I slid down, by a bottom of packthread, into
the street, and so 'scaped. But, sir, thus much I can assure
you, for I heard it while I was locked up, there were a great 40
many rich merchants, and brave citizens' wives with 'em at
a feast, and your son, Master Edward, withdrew with one
of 'em, and has 'pointed to meet her anon, at one Cob's
house, a water-bearer that dwells by the wall. Now, there
your worship shall be sure to take him, for there he preys,   45
and fail he will not.

KNOWELL

Nor will I fail, to break his match, I doubt not.
Go thou along with Justice Clement's man,
And stay there for me. At one Cob's house, say'st thou?

BRAINWORM

Aye, sir, there you shall have him.   50

[*Exit* KNOWELL]

Yes? Invisible? Much wench, or much son! 'Slight, when he
has stayed there, three or four hours, travailing with the
expectation of wonders, and at length be delivered of air;

---

30 *seemed men* i.e. showed their aggressive side
35 *anatomy* a dissected body
38 *bottom of packthread* ball or skein of stout twine
41 *brave* finely-dressed
41–2 *rich ... feast* Seeking to avoid the implication of adultery (in citizens' wives
     dining surreptitiously with merchants), Jackson repunctuates this line as 'rich
     merchants' and brave citizens' wives with 'em at a feast' – quite plausibly, since
     Jonson tended to overuse commas and omit apostrophes. But Jonson was evi-
     dently not as decorous as Jackson supposes: during the War of the Theatres,
     Thomas Dekker's *Satiromastix* accused Jonson of mocking 'worshipful citizens'
     and calling their 'modest and virtuous wives punks and cockatrices' (1602
     Quarto, sig. I3v).
44 *the wall* London's old City wall
47 *match* appointment; also, matrimonial alliance (OED)
51 *Much wench, or much son* i.e. He's likely to find a wench and his son (spoken
     sarcastically, since he knows that Knowell will not find 'much' of anyone)
52–3 *travailing ... air* i.e. in labour, but finally giving birth to nothing

oh, the sport that I should then take, to look on him, if I
durst! But now I mean to appear no more afore him in this   55
shape. I have another trick to act yet. Oh, that I were so
happy as to light on a nupson, now, of this Justice's novice.
[*To* FORMAL] Sir, I make you stay somewhat long.

FORMAL
Not a whit, sir. 'Pray you, what do you mean? Sir?

BRAINWORM
I was putting up some papers –   60

FORMAL
You ha' been lately in the wars, sir, it seems.

BRAINWORM
Marry have I, sir; to my loss; and expense of all, almost –

FORMAL
Troth, sir, I would be glad to bestow a pottle of wine o'
you, if it please you to accept it –

BRAINWORM
Oh, sir –   65

FORMAL
But to hear the manner of your services, and your devices
in the wars, they say they be very strange, and not like those
a man reads in the Roman histories, or sees at Mile End.

BRAINWORM
No, I assure you, sir; why, at any time when it please you,
I shall be ready to discourse to you, all I know; [*Aside*] and   70
more too, somewhat.

FORMAL
No better time than now, sir: we'll go to the Windmill;
there we shall have a cup of neat grist, we call it. I pray you,
sir, let me request you to the Windmill.

BRAINWORM
I'll follow you, sir, [*Aside*] and make grist o' you, if I have   75
good luck.

[*Exeunt*]

56–7 *Oh, that ... novice* i.e. Oh, how I wish I could now have the good luck to find
   a gullible fool in this young assistant of Justice Clement
63 *pottle* vessel containing about two quarts
68 *Mile End* See II.iii.141–2n.
73 *neat* undiluted
   grist malt crushed or ground for brewing (OED); here used for strong beer made
   from grist
75 *make grist o' you* i.e. either (1) reap profit or advantage from you (cf. the saying,
   'all is grist that comes to his mill', OED grist *sb.*² 2.c); or (2) crush you

Act IV, Scene v

[*Enter*] MATTHEW, EDWARD, BOBADILL [*and*] STEPHEN

MATTHEW
Sir, did your eyes ever taste the like clown of him, where we
were today, Master Wellbred's half-brother? I think the
whole earth cannot show his parallel, by this daylight.

EDWARD
We were now speaking of him: Captain Bobadill tells me he
is fall'n foul o' you, too.   5

MATTHEW
Oh, aye, sir, he threatened me with the *bastinado*.

BOBADILL
Aye, but I think I taught you prevention, this morning, for
that – You shall kill him, beyond question; if you be so generously minded.

MATTHEW
Indeed, it is a most excellent trick! (*Practices at a post*)   10

BOBADILL
Oh, you do not give spirit enough to your motion, you are
too tardy, too heavy! Oh, it must be done like lightning:
hai!

MATTHEW
Rare, Captain!

BOBADILL
Tut, 'tis nothing an't be not done in a – *punto*!   15

EDWARD
Captain, did you ever prove yourself upon any of our
masters of defence, here?

MATTHEW
Oh, good sir! Yes, I hope, he has.

Act IV, Scene v This is IV.vii in F.

  1 *taste the like clown of him* i.e. see such an ignorant boor as Downright

  6 *bastinado* See I.iv.93n.

  7 *prevention* defence

  8–9 *generously* nobly, gallantly, bravely (OED)

 13 *hai!* exclamation made upon hitting an opponent (Italian for 'you have [it]'); F
    reads 'hay?'

 15 *punto* either (1) moment, instant; or (2) a stroke or thrust with the point of the
    sword or foil (OED)

 16 *prove* try, test

 18 *hope* suppose, think (OED); i.e. I should think so (as an emphatic); presumably
    Matthew has already heard this story.

BOBADILL

I will tell you, sir. Upon my first coming to the City, after
my long travail for knowledge (in that mystery only), there   20
came three or four of 'em to me, at a gentleman's house,
where it was my chance to be resident at that time, to
entreat my presence at their schools, and withal so much
importuned me that (I protest to you as I am a gentleman)
I was ashamed of their rude demeanour, out of all measure.   25
Well, I told 'em that to come to a public school, they should
pardon me, it was opposite (in diameter) to my humour,
but, if so they would give their attendance at my lodging, I
protested to do them what right or favour I could, as I was
a gentleman, and so forth.   30

EDWARD

So, sir, then you tried their skill?

BOBADILL

Alas, soon tried! You shall hear sir. Within two or three
days after, they came; and, by honesty, fair sir, believe me,
I graced them exceedingly, showed them some two or three
tricks of prevention have purchased 'em, since, a credit, to   35
admiration! They cannot deny this; and yet now, they hate
me, and why? Because I am excellent, and for no other vile
reason on the earth.

EDWARD

This is strange, and barbarous, as ever I heard!

BOBADILL

Nay, for a more instance of their preposterous natures, but   40
note, sir. They have assaulted me some three, four, five, six
of them together, as I have walked alone, in divers skirts i'
the town, as Turnbull, Whitechapel, Shoreditch, which
were then my quarters, and since upon the Exchange, at my
lodging, and at my ordinary; where I have driven them   45
afore me, the whole length of a street, in the open view of

19–54 *I will tell you ... multitudes* Bobadill's story resembles claims made by
Italian fencing-masters about defeating their jealous and ruthless Elizabethan
English competitors; the play supports the Englishmen's side of the story, in
which (even without swords) they battered their pretentious, cowardly rivals.

20 *travail* labour (also, travel)

mystery craft, art, profession, or calling

35–6 *have ... admiration* i.e. that have won them a spectacular reputation

40 *preposterous* perverse, ungrateful, outrageous

42 *skirts* outskirts; suburbs

43 *Turnbull ... Shoreditch* Bobadill neglects to conceal that he has lived in these
very unfashionable districts.

45 *ordinary* eating-house or tavern

all our gallants, pitying to hurt them, believe me. Yet, all
this lenity will not o'ercome their spleen: they will be doing
with the pismire, raising a hill a man may spurn abroad,
with his foot, at pleasure. By myself, I could have slain   50
them all, but I delight not in murder. I am loath to bear any
other than this *bastinado* for 'em; yet, I hold it good polity
not to go disarmed, for though I be skilful, I may be
oppressed with multitudes.

EDWARD

Aye, believe me, may you sir; and (in my conceit) our whole   55
nation should sustain the loss by it, if it were so.

BOBADILL

Alas, no: what's a peculiar man, to a nation? Not seen.

EDWARD

Oh, but your skill, sir!

BOBADILL

Indeed, that might be some loss; but, who respects it? I will
tell you, sir, by the way of private, and under seal; I am a   60
gentleman, and live here obscure, and to myself; but, were
I known to Her Majesty and the Lords (observe me) I
would undertake (upon this poor head, and life), for the
public benefit of the state, not only to spare the entire lives
of her subjects in general, but to save the one half, nay,   65
three parts of her yearly charge in holding war, and against
what enemy soever. And, how would I do it, think you?

EDWARD

Nay, I know not, nor can I conceive.

BOBADILL

Why, thus, sir. I would select nineteen more, to myself,
throughout the land: gentlemen they should be of good   70
spirit, strong, and able constitution, I would choose them
by an instinct, a character, that I have; and I would teach
these nineteen the special rules, as your *punto*, your
reverso, your *stoccata*, your *imbroccata*, your *passada*,

---

48 *spleen* envy
49 *pismire* ant   *spurn abroad* kick aside
52 *polity* policy
55 *conceit* judgement or estimation
57 *peculiar* individual
60 *by the way ... under seal* privately, and as a secret
66 *charge* expense
74 *reverso* back-blow (OED)
    stoccata See I.iv.107n.
    imbroccata 'a pass or thrust', especially one 'given over the dagger'
    passada See I.iv.136n.

your *montanto*; till they could all play very near, or   75
altogether as well as myself. This done, say the enemy were
forty thousand strong, we twenty would come into the
field, the tenth of March, or thereabouts; and we would
challenge twenty of the enemy; they could not, in their
honour, refuse us; well, we would kill them; challenge   80
twenty more, kill them; twenty more, kill them; twenty
more, kill them too; and thus would we kill, every man, his
twenty a day, that's twenty score; twenty score, that's two
hundred; two hundred a day, five days a thousand; forty
thousand; forty times five, five times forty, two hundred   85
days kills them all up, by computation. And this will I venture my poor gentleman-like carcass to perform (provided
there be no treason practised upon us) by fair and discreet
manhood, that is, civilly by the sword.

EDWARD
Why, are you so sure of your hand, Captain, at all times?   90

BOBADILL
Tut, never miss thrust, upon my reputation with you.

EDWARD
I would not stand in Downright's state, then, an' you meet
him, for the wealth of any one street in London.

BOBADILL
Why, sir, you mistake me! If he were here now, by this
welkin, I would not draw my weapon on him! Let this   95
gentleman do his mind; but, I will *bastinado* him (by the
bright sun) wherever I meet him.

MATTHEW
Faith, and I'll have a fling at him, at my distance.

EDWARD
God's so', look where he is: yonder he goes.

[DOWNRIGHT] *walks over the stage*

DOWNRIGHT
What peevish luck have I, I cannot meet with these brag-   100
ging rascals?

---

75 *montanto* a vertical thrust
83–4 *twenty score, that's two hundred* This mathematical error leads Bobadill to
    double the number of days required. Ridiculous though Bobadill's plan is on this
    scale, Jonson himself had challenged an enemy soldier to single combat and
    killed him a few years before writing this play.
92 *stand in Downright's state* i.e. trade places with Downright
95 *welkin* sky; heaven
96 *do his mind* do as he wishes

BOBADILL
    It's not he? Is it?
EDWARD
    Yes, faith, it is he.

                                                    [*Exit* DOWNRIGHT]

MATTHEW
    I'll be hanged, then, if that were he.
EDWARD
    Sir, keep your hanging good for some greater matter, for I   105
    assure you, that was he.
STEPHEN
    Upon my reputation, it was he.
BOBADILL
    Had I thought it had been he, he must not have gone so; but
    I can hardly be induced to believe it was he, yet.
EDWARD
    That I think, sir. But see, he is come again!   110

                          [*Enter* DOWNRIGHT]

DOWNRIGHT
    Oh, Pharaoh's foot, have I found you? Come, draw, to
    your tools: draw, gipsy, or I'll thrash you.
BOBADILL
    Gentleman of valour, I do believe in thee, hear me –
DOWNRIGHT
    Draw your weapon, then.
BOBADILL
    Tall man, I never thought on it till now (body of me): I had   115
    a warrant of the peace served on me, even now, as I came
    along, by a water-bearer; this gentleman saw it, Master
    Matthew.
DOWNRIGHT
    'Sdeath, you will not draw, then?

        He beats him, and disarms him; MATTHEW *runs away*

---

105 *keep your hanging good* i.e. (mockingly) preserve your hanging, keep it unim-
     paired for future use (since Matthew said he would be hanged if that were
     Downright, which it clearly was)
112 *tools* sword and dagger
     gipsy cunning rogue; OED does not find this meaning until 1627, but it appears
     earlier; perhaps also a pun on 'Egyptian', since Bobadill swears 'by the foot of
     Pharaoh' (Jackson).
115 *Tall* Brave, bold, valiant (OED)

BOBADILL

Hold, hold, under thy favour, forbear.   120

DOWNRIGHT

Prate again, as you like this, you whoreson foist, you.
You'll control the point, you? Your consort is gone? Had
he stayed, he had shared with you, sir.   [*Exit*]

BOBADILL

Well, gentlemen, bear witness, I was bound to the peace, by
this good day.   125

EDWARD

No, faith, it's an ill day, Captain, never reckon it other; but
say you were bound to the peace, the law allows you to
defend yourself: that'll prove but a poor excuse.

BOBADILL

I cannot tell, sir. I desire good construction, in fair sort. I
never sustained the like disgrace (by heaven), sure I was   130
struck with a planet thence, for I had no power to touch my
weapon.

EDWARD

Aye, like enough, I have heard of many that have been
beaten under a planet: go, get you to a surgeon.

[*Exit* BOBADILL]

'Slid, an' these be your tricks, your *passadas*, and your   135
montantos, I'll none of them. Oh, manners! That this age
should bring forth such creatures! That nature should be at
leisure to make 'em! Come, coz.

STEPHEN

Mass, I'll ha' this cloak.

EDWARD

God's will, 'tis Downright's.   140

---

121 *foist* See IV.ii.16n.
122 *control the point* See I.iv.150n.
129 *construction* interpretation put upon conduct
131 *struck with a planet* A common astrological diagnosis at the time, meaning
     deprived 'of one of the faculties, as if by a physical blow' (OED strike *v.* 46) due
     to 'the supposed malign influence of an adverse planet; blasted' (OED planet-
     struck; cf. Tilley P389).
     thence from heaven
134 *beaten ... planet* Edward mockingly associates Bobadill's excuse with Roman
     Catholic priests beaten while wearing the chasuble, called a 'planet'.
136 *Oh, manners!* i.e. What a world! Edward's line is a standard translation of
     Cicero's 'O tempora, O mores'.

STEPHEN

Nay, it's mine now, another might have ta'en up, as well as
I; I'll wear it, so I will.

EDWARD

How an' he see it? He'll challenge it, assure yourself.

STEPHEN

Aye, but he shall not ha' it: I'll say I bought it.

EDWARD

Take heed you buy it not too dear, coz.   145

[*Exeunt*]

Act IV, Scene vi

[*Enter*] KITELY, WELLBRED, DAME KITELY,
[*and*] BRIDGET

KITELY

Now, trust me brother, you were much to blame,
T' incense his anger, and disturb the peace
Of my poor house, where there are sentinels
That every minute watch, to give alarms
Of civil war, without adjection   5
Of your assistance, or occasion.

WELLBRED

No harm done, brother, I warrant you: since there is no
harm done. Anger costs a man nothing; and a tall man is
never his own man, till he be angry. To keep his valour in
obscurity is to keep himself, as it were, in a cloak-bag.   10
What's a musician, unless he play? What's a tall man,
unless he fight? For, indeed, all this my wise brother stands
upon, absolutely; and that made me fall in with him so
resolutely.

DAME KITELY

Aye, but what harm might have come of it, brother?   15

---

143 *How an' ... assure yourself* i.e. What if Downright sees it? He'll demand it, you
    can be sure

Act IV, Scene vi This is IV.viii in F.

   5 *adjection* addition

   9 *his own man* fully himself

  13 *fall in with* agree, harmonize (OED); but since this conversation seems to con-
     cern the fight at Kitely's house, in which Wellbred defied Downright, it must be
     spoken as an extension of the sarcasm of the preceding sentences.

WELLBRED
  Might, sister? So, might the good warm clothes your hus-
  band wears be poisoned, for anything he knows; or the
  wholesome wine he drunk, even now, at the table –
KITELY
  [*Aside*] Now, God forbid: oh me. Now I remember,
  My wife drunk to me, last; and changed the cup;   20
  And bade me wear this cursed suit today.
  See if heav'n suffer murder undiscovered!
  [*To* BRIDGET] I feel me ill: give me some mithridate,
  Some mithridate and oil, good sister, fetch me;
  Oh, I am sick at heart! I burn, I burn.   25
  If you will save my life, go, fetch it me.
WELLBRED
  Oh, strange humour! My very breath has poisoned him.
BRIDGET
  Good brother, be content, what do you mean?
  The strength of these extreme conceits will kill you.
DAME KITELY
  Beshrew your heart-blood, brother Wellbred, now,   30
  For putting such a toy into his head.
WELLBRED
  Is a fit simile, a toy? Will he be poisoned with a simile?
  Brother Kitely, what a strange and idle imagination is this?
  For shame, be wiser. O' my soul, there's no such matter.
KITELY
  Am I not sick? How am I, then, not poisoned?   35
  Am I not poisoned? How am I, then, so sick?
DAME KITELY
  If you be sick, your own thoughts make you sick.
WELLBRED
  His jealousy is the poison he has taken.

22 *suffer* tolerate
23 *mithridate* a supposed universal antidote for poison
25 *sick at heart* Various meanings apply: sick to my stomach (cf. French *avoir mal
    au coeur*, to be bilious); suffering from chest pains, heartburn, etc.; melancholy
    or heartsick.
    I burn Jealousy was known as a burning mental state. Kitely may also be think-
    ing of Hercules, burned by poisoned clothing his wife gave him.
29 *extreme conceits* i.e. powerful conceptions; Bridget echoes a contemporary belief
    that imagining a poisoning so vividly might have the same effect as actual
    poison.
30 *Beshrew your heart-blood* A curse, similar to 'damn your eyes'.
31 *toy* fantasy (Dent-S T456.1)

[*Enter*] BRAINWORM. *He comes disguised like Justice*
Clement's man [*Formal*]

BRAINWORM
Master Kitely, my master, Justice Clement, salutes you; and
desires to speak with you, with all possible speed.   40
KITELY
No time but now? When, I think, I am sick? Very sick!
Well, I will wait upon his worship. Thomas! Cob! [*Aside*] I
must seek them out, and set 'em sentinels, till I return.
Thomas! Cob! Thomas!   [*Exit*]
WELLBRED
[*Takes* BRAINWORM *aside*] This is perfectly rare, Brain-   45
worm! But how got'st thou this apparel, of the Justice's
man?
BRAINWORM
Marry sir, my proper fine pen-man would needs bestow the
grist o' me, at the Windmill, to hear some martial discourse,
where so I marshalled him that I made him drunk with   50
admiration! And, because too much heat was the cause of
his distemper, I stripped him stark naked, as he lay along
asleep, and borrowed his suit, to deliver this counterfeit
message in, leaving a rusty armour and an old brown bill to
watch him, till my return; which shall be, when I ha'   55
pawned his apparel, and spent the better part o' the money,
perhaps.
WELLBRED
Well, thou art a successful merry knave, Brainworm, his
absence will be a good subject for more mirth. I pray thee,
return to thy young master, and will him to meet me, and   60
my sister Bridget, at the Tower instantly: for here, tell him,
the house is so stored with jealousy, there is no room for

48–9 *my proper fine ... Windmill* i.e. this oh-so admirable legal secretary insisted
    on buying me the products of the Windmill (the name of a tavern, but playing
    off the way windmills were used to grind grist); Jonson and Brainworm borrow
    the trick of stealing the costume from *The Merrie Conceited Jests of George
    Peele* and *The Blind Beggar of Bednal Green*.
51–2 *too much heat ... distemper* An ironically literal rendition of a standard diag-
    nosis in Renaissance humours theory.
54 *brown bill* a kind of halberd painted brown (OED); see III.iii.11n
61 *Tower* 'They could be married at once within the precincts of the Tower, which
    was extra-parochial' (H&S) – that is, an area called a 'liberty', free from some
    of the rules governing the City proper.

love to stand upright in. We must get our fortunes committed to some larger prison, say; and, than the Tower, I know
no better air; nor where the liberty of the house may do us   65
more present service. Away.

               [*Exit* BRAINWORM]

       [*Enter* KITELY *and* CASH]

KITELY
Come hither, Thomas. Now, my secret's ripe,
And thou shalt have it: lay to both thine ears.
Hark what I say to thee. I must go forth, Thomas.
Be careful of thy promise, keep good watch,   70
Note every gallant, and observe him well,
That enters in my absence, to thy mistress:
If she would show him rooms, the jest is stale,
Follow 'em, Thomas, or else hang on him,
And let him not go after; mark their looks;   75
Note if she offer but to see his band,
Or any other amorous toy, about him;
But praise his leg, or foot; or if she say,
The day is hot, and bid him feel her hand,
How hot it is: oh, that's a monstrous thing!   80
Note me all this, good Thomas, mark their sighs,
And, if they do but whisper, break 'em off:
I'll bear thee out in it. Wilt thou do this?
Wilt thou be true, my Thomas?
CASH   As truth's self, sir.

---

63 *stand upright* i.e. grow, and be honourable; but (like so many other remarks concerning Kitely's jealousy) with a possible secondary reference to penile erection
63–4 *committed to* incarcerated in, with a secondary sense of 'entrusted to'
65 *liberty of* unrestricted use of, or access to; permission to go anywhere within the
  limits of (OED), with the sense here of special privileges granted to inmates; but
  also referring to the Tower's convenient status as a 'liberty' (see the note to line
  61 above)
68 *lay to both thine ears* i.e. listen carefully
73 *show him rooms* give a tour of the house, but cf. the sexual implications of Tilley
  F594: 'lies backwards and lets out her forerooms'
  the jest is stale it's an old story (or trick); with a pun on the senses of 'stale' as
  'a deceptive means of allurement' and 'a prostitute'
76 *band* collar or ruff
77 *amorous toy* attractive trifle
79–80 *hand ... hot* Cf. *Othello* III.iv.36–43, where Othello finds Desdemona's
  hand 'Hot, hot and moist' and claims that 'here's a young and sweating devil
  here / That commonly rebels'.

KITELY

Why, I believe thee; where is Cob, now? Cob?   [*Exit*]   85

DAME KITELY

He's ever calling for Cob! I wonder how he employs Cob
so!

WELLBRED

Indeed, sister, to ask how he employs Cob is a necessary
question for you, that are his wife, and a thing not very easy
for you to be satisfied in; but this I'll assure you, Cob's wife   90
is an excellent bawd, sister, and oftentimes your husband
haunts her house, marry, to what end, I cannot altogether
accuse him, imagine you what you think convenient. But, I
have known fair hides have foul hearts ere now, sister.

DAME KITELY

Never said you truer than that, brother, so much I can tell   95
you for your learning. Thomas, fetch your cloak, and go
with me, I'll after him presently.

[*Exit* CASH]

I would to fortune I could take him there, i' faith. I'd return
him his own, I warrant him.   [*Exit*]

WELLBRED

So, let 'em go: this may make sport anon. Now, my fair   100
sister-in-law, that you knew but how happy a thing it were
to be fair and beautiful!

BRIDGET

That touches not me, brother.

WELLBRED

That's true; that's even the fault of it: for, indeed, beauty
stands a woman in no stead, unless it procure her touching.   105
But, sister, whether it touch you or no, it touches your
beauties; and I am sure they will abide the touch. An' they

---

91 *bawd* the madam of a brothel

92 *to what end* for what purpose

94 *fair hides have foul hearts* Cf. Tilley F29: 'fair face, foul heart'

98–9 *I would ... warrant him* i.e. I wish for the luck to catch him there, I swear. I'd
    pay him back, he can be sure of that

103 *touches not* i.e. has no relevance to

105 *stands a woman ... touching* i.e. does a woman no good unless it provokes men
    to touch her

107 *abide the touch* Various senses apply, simultaneously: tolerate physical contact;
    pass the test (gold and silver were tested by rubbing on a touchstone); submit to
    the application of cosmetics.

do not, a plague of all ceruse, say I; and it touches me too
in part, though not in the – Well, there's a dear and
respected friend of mine, sister, stands very strongly, and 110
worthily affected toward you, and hath vowed to inflame
whole bonfires of zeal, at his heart, in honour of your per-
fections. I have already engaged my promise to bring you
where you shall hear him confirm much more. Ned
Knowell is the man, sister. There's no exception against the 115
party. You are ripe for a husband; and a minute's loss to
such an occasion is a great trespass in a wise beauty. What
say you, sister? On my soul he loves you. Will you give him
the meeting?

BRIDGET
Faith, I had very little confidence in mine own constancy, 120
brother, if I durst not meet a man; but this motion of yours
savours of an old knight-adventurer's servant a little too
much, methinks.

WELLBRED
What's that, sister?

BRIDGET
Marry, of the squire.   125

WELLBRED
No matter if it did, I would be such an one for my friend,
but see! Who is returned to hinder us?

[*Enter* KITELY]

KITELY
What villainy is this? Called out on a false message? This
was some plot! I was not sent for. Bridget, where's your
sister?   130

BRIDGET
I think she be gone forth, sir.

KITELY
How! Is my wife gone forth? Whither, for God's sake?

---

108 *ceruse* a paint or cosmetic for the skin (OED); from the name for white lead.
   Wellbred teases Bridget that, if her beauty does not stand up to touching, she
   should curse her cosmetics for smudging too easily

109 *in the* – Omission of the word 'whole' points to a bawdy play on 'hole', slang for
   various bodily orifices.

112 *bonfires* large celebratory fires, but with a commonplace play on 'bone-fires' –
   venereal disease, often called 'the bone-ache'

115–16 *exception against the party* objection to the person

121–2 *this motion of yours savours of* i.e. this suggestion or little play of yours
   reminds me of

125 *squire* Bridget alludes to an 'apple-squire', a pimp; cf. IV.viii.58.

BRIDGET
  She's gone abroad with Thomas.
KITELY
  Abroad with Thomas? Oh, that villain dors me.
  He hath discovered all unto my wife!   135
  Beast that I was to trust him; whither, I pray you, went she?
BRIDGET
  I know not, sir.
WELLBRED
  I'll tell you, brother, whither I suspect she's gone.
KITELY
  Whither, good brother?
WELLBRED
  To Cob's house, I believe; but, keep my counsel.   140
KITELY
  I will, I will; to Cob's house? Doth she haunt Cob's?
  She's gone a' purpose, now, to cuckold me,
  With that lewd rascal, who, to win her favour,
  Hath told her all.   [*Exit*]
WELLBRED   Come, he's once more gone.
  Sister, let's lose no time: th' affair is worth it.   145

                                          [*Exeunt*]

Act IV, Scene vii

[*Enter*] MATTHEW [*and*] BOBADILL

MATTHEW
  I wonder, Captain, what they will say of my going away?
  Ha?
BOBADILL
  Why, what should they say, but as of a discreet gentleman?
  Quick, wary, respectful of nature's fair lineaments; and
  that's all.   5
MATTHEW
  Why, so! But what can they say of your beating?
BOBADILL
  A rude part, a touch with soft wood, a kind of gross bat-

---

134 *dors* makes a fool of (OED)
135 *discovered* revealed
140 *counsel* secret

Act IV, Scene vii This is IV.ix in F.
  7 *part* piece of conduct

tery used, laid on strongly, borne most patiently; and that's
all.

MATTHEW

Aye, but would any man have offered it in Venice, as you   10
say?

BOBADILL

Tut, I assure you, no: you shall have there your *Nobilis*,
your *Gentilezza*, come in bravely upon your *reverse*, stand
you close, stand you firm, stand you fair, save your *retricato* with his left leg, come to the *assalto* with the right,   15
thrust with brave steel, defy your base wood! But wherefore
do I awake this remembrance? I was fascinated, by Jupiter,
fascinated; but I will be unwitched, and revenged, by law.

MATTHEW

Do you hear? Is't not best to get a warrant, and have him
arrested, and brought before Justice Clement?   20

BOBADILL

It were not amiss: would we had it.

[*Enter*] BRAINWORM [*disguised as Justice Clement's
man Formal*]

MATTHEW

Why, here comes his man, let's speak to him.

BOBADILL

Agreed, do you speak.

MATTHEW

Save you, sir.

BRAINWORM

With all my heart, sir.   25

MATTHEW

Sir, there is one Downright hath abused this gentleman, and
myself, and we determine to make our amends by law;
now, if you would do us the favour to procure a warrant,
to bring him afore your master, you shall be well considered, I assure you, sir.   30

BRAINWORM

Sir, you know my service is my living: such favours as these,

---

12 *Tut* i.e. Nonsense
   Nobilis nobles (Latin); or a mistake for the Italian word *nobili*
13 *Gentilezza* gentry
14–15 *retricato* no such word is known; H&S suggests that Bobadill may be thinking of *rintricato*, 'entangled'.
15 *assalto* assault
17 *fascinated* bewitched

gotten of my master, is his only preferment; and therefore
you must consider me, as I may make benefit of my place.

MATTHEW

How is that, sir?

BRAINWORM

Faith, sir, the thing is extraordinary, and the gentleman   35
may be of great accompt; yet, be what he will, if you will
lay me down a brace of angels in my hand, you shall have
it, otherwise not.

MATTHEW

How shall we do, Captain? He asks a brace of angels, you
have no money?   40

BOBADILL

Not a cross, by fortune.

MATTHEW

Nor I, as I am a gentleman, but two pence, left of my two
shillings in the morning for wine and radish: let's find him
some pawn.

BOBADILL

Pawn? We have none to the value of his demand.   45

MATTHEW

Oh, yes. I'll pawn this jewel in my ear, and you may pawn
your silk stockings, and pull up your boots, they will ne'er
be missed; it must be done now.

BOBADILL

Well, an' there be no remedy; I'll step aside, and pull 'em
off.   50

MATTHEW

Do you hear, sir? We have no store of money at this time,
but you shall have good pawns: look you, sir, this jewel,
and that gentleman's silk stockings, because we would have
it dispatched ere we went to our chambers.

BRAINWORM

I am content, sir: I will get you the warrant presently;   55
what's his name, say you? Downright?

MATTHEW

Aye, aye, George Downright.

BRAINWORM

What manner of man is he?

---

32 *his only preferment* the only income or career opportunity he gives me

36 *accompt* account, stature

37 *brace of angels* a pair of the gold coins; Brainworm takes advantage of their
     terror of Downright to impose an exorbitant charge for this legal service.

41 *cross* a coin, either penny or halfpenny, marked with a cross

MATTHEW
  A tall big man, sir; he goes in a cloak, most commonly, of
  silk russet, laid about with russet lace.   60
BRAINWORM
  'Tis very good, sir.
MATTHEW
  Here sir, here's my jewel.
BOBADILL
  And, here, are stockings.
BRAINWORM
  Well, gentlemen, I'll procure you this warrant presently,
  but who will you have to serve it?   65
MATTHEW
  That's true, Captain; that must be considered.
BOBADILL
  Body o' me, I know not! 'Tis service of danger!
BRAINWORM
  Why, you were best get one o' the varlets o' the City, a
  sergeant. I'll appoint you one, if you please.
MATTHEW
  Will you, sir? Why, we can wish no better.   70
BOBADILL
  We'll leave it to you, sir.

                    [*Exeunt* BOBADILL *and* MATTHEW]

BRAINWORM
  This is rare! Now will I go pawn this cloak of the Justice's
  man's at the brokers for a varlet's suit, and be the varlet
  myself; and get either more pawns, or more money of
  Downright, for the arrest.   [*Exit*] 75

Act IV, Scene viii

                    [*Enter*] KNOWELL

KNOWELL
  Oh, here it is, I am glad: I have found it now. Ho! Who is
  within, here?

  60 *silk russet ... russet lace* Russet could refer to either a reddish colour or a coarse
     fabric; the red might reflect Downright's angry 'humour', the coarseness his
     assertive rustic plainness.
  68 *varlets* not pejorative here: synonymous with 'sergeants', officers charged with
     the arrest of offenders or the summoning of persons to appear before the court
     (OED)
  Act IV, Scene viii This is IV.x in F.

TIB
  I am within sir, what's your pleasure?
KNOWELL
  To know who is within, besides yourself.
TIB
  Why, sir, you are no constable, I hope?   5
KNOWELL
  Oh! Fear you the constable? Then, I doubt not.
  You have some guests within deserve that fear,
  I'll fetch him straight.

[TIB *opens the door*]

TIB   O' God's name, sir.
KNOWELL
  Go to. Come, tell me, is not young Knowell here?
TIB
  Young Knowell? I know none such, sir, o' mine honesty!   10
KNOWELL
  Your honesty? Dame, it flies too lightly from you;
  There is no way but, fetch the constable.
TIB
  The constable? The man is mad, I think. [*Closes the door*]

[*Enter* DAME KITELY *and* CASH]

CASH
  Ho, who keeps house here?
KNOWELL
  Oh, this is the female copesmate of my son!   15
  Now shall I meet him straight.
DAME KITELY   Knock, Thomas, hard.
CASH
  Ho, good wife?

[*Enter* TIB]

TIB   Why, what's the matter with you?
DAME KITELY
  Why, woman, grieves it you to ope your door?
  Belike you get something to keep it shut.
TIB
  What mean these questions, pray ye?   20

---

  8 *O' God's name* For God's sake
 15 *copesmate* companion, but drawing on the sexual sense of the verb 'to cope' (cf.
       Othello IV.i.86, 'to cope your wife')
 19 *Belike ... shut* i.e. You probably get paid to guard it: you are a bawd

DAME KITELY
  So strange you make it? Is not my husband here?
KNOWELL
  Her husband!
DAME KITELY
  My tried husband, Master Kitely.
TIB
  I hope he needs not to be tried here.
DAME KITELY
  No, dame: he does it not for need, but pleasure.   25
TIB
  Neither for need, nor pleasure, is he here.
KNOWELL
  This is but a device, to balk me withal.

                    [*Enter* KITELY]

  Soft, who is this? 'Tis not my son, disguised?
DAME KITELY
  (Spies her husband come, and runs to him)
  Oh, sir, have I forestalled your honest market?
  Found your close walks? You stand amazed, now, do you?   30
  I' faith, I am glad, I have smoked you yet at last!
  What is your jewel, trow? In; come, let's see her
  (Fetch forth your huswife, dame): if she be fairer,
  In any honest judgement, than myself,
  I'll be content with it; but, she is change,   35
  She feeds you fat, she soothes your appetite,
  And you are well? Your wife, an honest woman,
  Is meat twice sod to you, sir? Oh, you treacher!
KNOWELL
  She cannot counterfeit thus palpably.

---

21 *So strange you make it?* i.e. You pretend not to know what I'm talking about?
23 *tried* refined, excellent (here spoken sarcastically)
24 *tried* Several senses may apply: to be put on trial, to have fluids extracted, and
   to be solicited sexually. OED does not find this third usage before 1713, but
   Jackson points out Shakespeare's *The Passionate Pilgrim*, Sonnet 11, lines 3–4.
27 *a device, to balk me withal* i.e. a trick to hinder me
28 *Soft* An exclamation to himself, meaning, wait a minute, be quietly observant.
29 *forestalled ... market* literally, prevented sales at a market ... by dissuading persons from bringing in their goods (OED); here the commerce is sexual
30 *close* hidden, secret (OED)
31 *smoked* smoked out, as a fox from its hole (cf. Tilley S577)
33 *huswife* whore
38 *twice sod* stale, unpalatable; literally, boiled twice (OED; cf. Tilley C511)
   treacher deceiver, cheat (OED)

KITELY

   Out on thy more-than-strumpet's impudence!   40
   Steal'st thou thus to thy haunts? And have I taken
   Thy bawd, and thee, and thy companion, (*Pointing to*
      KNOWELL)
   This hoary-headed lecher, this old goat,
   Close at your villainy, and would'st thou 'scuse it,
   With this stale harlot's jest, accusing me?   45
   (*To him*) Oh, old incontinent, dost not thou shame,
   When all thy powers' inchastity is spent,
   To have a mind so hot? And to entice,
   And feed th' enticements of a lustful woman?

DAME KITELY

   Out, I defy thee, I, dissembling wretch!   50

KITELY

   Defy me, strumpet. Ask thy pander, here, [*Pointing to*
      CASH]
   Can he deny it? Or that wicked elder?

KNOWELL

   Why, hear you, sir.

KITELY   Tut, tut, tut: never speak.
   Thy guilty conscience will discover thee.

KNOWELL

   What lunacy is this, that haunts this man?   55

KITELY

   Well, good wife B-A-'-D, Cob's wife; and you,
   That make your husband such a hoddy-doddy;

40–1 *Out on ... haunts?* i.e. Damn your worse-than-whore's nerve! Is this how you
    sneak to your hangouts?

43 *goat* Conventionally associated with perpetual lustfulness; cf. Tilley G167: 'lech-
    erous as a goat'.

45 *stale ... me* i.e. tired old whore's trick of accusing me instead

46 *incontinent* unable to contain oneself, generally referring, in the Renaissance, to
    a lack of sexual discipline

47 *powers' ... spent* i.e. wayward sexual capabilities are gone; F reads 'powers in
    chastity', which does not fit with Kitely's line of accusation. Lever and Jackson
    therefore propose this emendation, with the partial authority of Q, which reads
    'powers inchastity' (and the absence of possessive apostrophes meant little in
    Elizabethan orthography).

51 *pander* pimp

53 *hear you* i.e. listen to me

56 *B-A-'-D* Kitely is calling Tib at once a bad wife and a bawd, with perhaps a sug-
    gestion also of the sound of a goat.

57 *hoddy-doddy* literally, a small shell-snail; the snail's 'horns' account for the sense
    here of 'cuckold' (OED).

And you, young apple-squire; and old cuckold-maker;
I'll ha' you every one before a justice:
Nay, you shall answer it, I charge you go.   60
KNOWELL
Marry, with all my heart, sir: I go willingly.
Though I do taste this as a trick, put on me
To punish my impertinent search – and justly;
And half forgive my son for the device.
KITELY
Come, will you go?
DAME KITELY   Go? To thy shame, believe it.   65

[*Enter* COB]

COB
Why, what's the matter here? What's here to do?
KITELY
Oh, Cob, art thou come? I have been abused,
And i' thy house. Never was man so wronged!
COB
'Slid, in my house, my master Kitely? Who wrongs you in
my house?   70
KITELY
Marry, young lust in old; and old in young, here:
Thy wife's their bawd, here have I taken 'em.
COB
How? Bawd? Is my house come to that? Am I preferred
thither?

Falls upon his wife and beats her

Did I charge you to keep your doors shut, Is'bel? And do   75
you let 'em lie open for all comers?
KNOWELL
Friend, know some cause before thou beat'st thy wife,
This's madness in thee.
COB   Why? Is there no cause?
KITELY
Yes, I'll show cause before the Justice, Cob:
Come, let her go with me.
COB   Nay, she shall go.   80

58 *apple-squire* pimp
73–4 *preferred thither* 'advanced' to the status of bawd
74 s.d. *Falls upon* Takes hold of
75 *Is'bel* The name would have been similar in sound to 'Jezebel', name of the
   'painted' queen of Ahab in the Old Testament, and a byword for 'whore'.

TIB

Nay, I will go. I'll see an' you may be allowed to make a bundle o' hemp o' your right and lawful wife thus, at every cuckoldly knave's pleasure. Why do you not go?

KITELY

A bitter quean. Come, we'll ha' you tamed.

[*Exeunt*]

Act IV, Scene ix

[*Enter*] BRAINWORM [*disguised as a City sergeant*]

BRAINWORM

Well, of all my disguises yet, now am I most like myself, being in this sergeant's gown. A man of my present profession never counterfeits, till he lays hold upon a debtor, and says, he 'rests him, for then he brings him to all manner of unrest. A kind of little kings we are, bearing the diminutive   5
of a mace, made like a young artichoke, that always carries pepper and salt in itself. Well, I know not what danger I undergo by this exploit; pray heaven, I come well off.

[*Enter* MATTHEW *and* BOBADILL]

MATTHEW

See, I think yonder is the varlet, by his gown.

BOBADILL

Let's go in quest of him.   10

MATTHEW

'Save you, friend, are not you here by appointment of Justice Clement's man?

BRAINWORM

Yes, an't please you, sir: he told me two gentlemen had willed him to procure a warrant from his master, which I have about me, to be served on one Downright.   15

---

82 *hemp* Hemp stems were beaten in the process of making rope.
84 *quean* whore

Act IV, Scene ix This is IV.xi in F.

   4 *'rests* arrests
   6 *mace* Originally 'a heavy staff or club ... often spiked'; here 'a sceptre or staff of office, resembling in shape the weapon of war'. Mace was also a spice, allowing Brainworm to play on the 'pepper and salt' the sergeant has the power to impose; Brainworm's trick here has a precedent in *The Black Bookes Messenger*.

MATTHEW
It is honestly done of you both; and see where the party
comes you must arrest. Serve it upon him, quickly, afore he
be aware –

[*Enter* STEPHEN *in Downright's cloak*]

BOBADILL
Bear back, Master Matthew.
BRAINWORM
Master Downright, I arrest you, i' the Queen's name, and   20
must carry you afore a Justice, by virtue of this warrant.
STEPHEN
Me, friend? I am no Downright, I, I am Master Stephen,
you do not well to arrest me, I tell you, truly: I am in
nobody's bonds, nor books, I, would you should know it.
A plague on you heartily, for making me thus afraid afore   25
my time.
BRAINWORM
Why, now are you deceived, gentlemen?
BOBADILL
He wears such a cloak, and that deceived us; but see, here
'a comes, indeed! This is he, officer.

[*Enter* DOWNRIGHT]

DOWNRIGHT
Why, how now, Signior Gull! Are you turned filcher of   30
late? Come, deliver my cloak.
STEPHEN
Your cloak, sir? I bought it, even now, in open market.
BRAINWORM
Master Downright, I have a warrant I must serve upon you,
procured by these two gentlemen.
DOWNRIGHT
These gentlemen? These rascals? [*Raises his cudgel*]   35
BRAINWORM
Keep the peace, I charge you, in Her Majesty's name.
DOWNRIGHT
I obey thee. What must I do, officer?
BRAINWORM
Go before Master Justice Clement, to answer what they can
object against you, sir. I will use you kindly, sir.

---

19 *Bear back* Retreat; probably an occasion to show Bobadill's fear of Downright
24 *bonds, nor books* places where actionable debt would be recorded; cf. Tilley
   B534

MATTHEW

Come, let's before, and make the Justice, Captain –   40

BOBADILL

The varlet's a tall man, afore heaven!

[*Exeunt* MATTHEW *and* BOBADILL]

DOWNRIGHT

Gull, you'll gi' me my cloak?

STEPHEN

Sir, I bought it, and I'll keep it.

DOWNRIGHT

You will.

STEPHEN

Aye, that I will.   45

DOWNRIGHT

[*Gives* BRAINWORM *money*] Officer, there's thy fee, arrest
him.

BRAINWORM

Master Stephen, I must arrest you.

STEPHEN

Arrest me, I scorn it. There, take your cloak, I'll none on't.

DOWNRIGHT

Nay, that shall not serve your turn now, sir. Officer, I'll go   50
with thee to the Justice's; bring him along.

STEPHEN

Why, is not here your cloak? What would you have?

DOWNRIGHT

I'll ha' you answer it, sir.

BRAINWORM

Sir, I'll take your word; and this gentleman's, too, for his
appearance.   55

DOWNRIGHT

I'll ha' no words taken. Bring him along.

BRAINWORM

Sir, I may choose to do that: I may take bail.

DOWNRIGHT

'Tis true, you may take bail, and choose – at another time;
but you shall not now, varlet. Bring him along, or I'll
swinge you. [*Raises his cudgel*]   60

---

40 *let's … Justice* i.e. let's go ahead of them and make our case to Justice Clement
53 *answer it* i.e. answer for it, be held responsible
54–5 *for his appearance* i.e. that he will appear for trial; Brainworm is trying to get
   out of delivering his prisoners personally to Justice Clement, since he has made
   the arrests under false pretences.
60 *swinge* beat

BRAINWORM
Sir, I pity the gentleman's case. Here's your money again.
DOWNRIGHT
'Sdeynes, tell not me of my money, bring him away, I say.
BRAINWORM
I warrant you he will go with you of himself, sir.
DOWNRIGHT
Yet more ado?
BRAINWORM
[*Aside*] I have made a fair mash on't.   65
STEPHEN
Must I go?
BRAINWORM
I know no remedy, Master Stephen.
DOWNRIGHT
Come along, afore me, here. I do not love your hanging
look behind.
STEPHEN
Why, sir, I hope you cannot hang me for it. Can he, fellow?   70
BRAINWORM
I think not, sir. It is but a whipping matter, sure!
STEPHEN
Why, then, let him do his worst, I am resolute.

                                                    [*Exeunt*]

Act V, Scene i

[*Enter*] CLEMENT, KNOWELL, KITELY, DAME KITELY,
TIB, CASH, COB [*and*] SERVANTS

CLEMENT
Nay, but stay, stay, give me leave; my chair, sirrah. You,
Master Knowell, say you went thither to meet your son.
KNOWELL
Aye, sir.
CLEMENT
But who directed you thither?
KNOWELL
That did mine own man, sir.   5

65 *mash* mess, 'hash'
68–9 *I do not … behind* both, I don't trust you lingering behind (because you may
    try to escape), and I don't like someone with your sour (or doomed, which
    Stephen picks up on) expression behind my back

CLEMENT
  Where is he?
KNOWELL
  Nay, I know not, now: I left him with your clerk, and
  appointed him to stay here for me.
CLEMENT
  My clerk? About what time was this?
KNOWELL
  Marry, between one and two, as I take it.   10
CLEMENT
  And, what time came my man with the false message to
  you, Master Kitely?
KITELY
  After two, sir.
CLEMENT
  Very good; but, Mistress Kitely, how that you were at
  Cob's? Ha?   15
DAME KITELY
  An' please you, sir, I'll tell you: my brother, Wellbred, told
  me that Cob's house was a suspected place –
CLEMENT
  So it appears, methinks; but, on.
DAME KITELY
  And that my husband used thither, daily.
CLEMENT
  No matter, so he used himself well, mistress.   20
DAME KITELY
  True sir, but you know what grows by such haunts, often-
  times.
CLEMENT
  I see rank fruits of a jealous brain, Mistress Kitely; but, did
  you find your husband there, in that case, as you suspected?
KITELY
  I found her there, sir.   25

7–8 *Nay ... for me* These lines are set as verse in F, with a line-break after 'clerk',
  but neither line is pentameter.
19 *used thither* i.e. made a habit of going there
20 *used* conducted or comported (OED)
25 *I found her there* Arthur Murphy's 1801 review describes the 'sharp eager tone'
  with which the most famous performer of Kitely interrupted here: 'He who
  remembers how Garrick uttered these words, slapping his hand on the table, as
  if he had made an important discovery, must acknowledge, trifling as it may now
  be thought, that it was a genuine stroke of nature....'

CLEMENT
  Did you so? That alters the case. Who gave you knowledge,
  of your wife's being there?
KITELY
  Marry, that did my brother Wellbred.
CLEMENT
  How? Wellbred first tell her? Then tell you, after? Where is
  Wellbred?   30
KITELY
  Gone with my sister, sir, I know not whither.
CLEMENT
  Why, this is a mere trick, a device: you are gulled in this
  most grossly, all! Alas, poor wench, wert thou beaten for
  this?
TIB
  Yes, most pitifully, an't please you.   35
COB
  And worthily, I hope: if it shall prove so.
CLEMENT
  Aye, that's like, and a piece of a sentence.

                    [*Enter a* SERVANT]

  How now, sir? What's the matter?
SERVANT
  Sir, there's a gentleman, i' the court without, desires to
  speak with your worship.   40
CLEMENT
  A gentleman? What's he?
SERVANT
  A soldier, sir, he says.
CLEMENT
  A soldier? Take down my armour, my sword, quickly: a

---

26 *That ... case* 'The case is altered' was proverbial (Tilley C111); it was also the
   title of Jonson's earliest known play (1597).
36 *worthily ... prove so* i.e. deservedly, if she behaved as immorally as I suspected
37 *like* likely (ironic)
   piece ... sentence i.e. fragment of sententious wisdom; possibly also, part of a
   legal judgement
43–7 *A soldier ... soldier enter* Probably inspired by an anecdote published in 1595:
   'A soldier coming about a suit to a merry Recorder of London, the Recorder ...
   ran hastily ... put on a corslet and head-piece, & then with a lance in his hand
   came down unto him, and said: How now Sirrah, are you the man that hath
   somewhat to say to me? Begin now when you dare, for behold (I trow) I am sufficiently provided for you' (Antony Copley, *Wits, Fits, and Fancies*; quoted by
   H&S).

soldier speak with me! Why, when, knaves? (*He arms him-*
self) Come on, come on, hold my cap there, so; give me my   45
gorget, my sword. Stand by, I will end your matters anon –
Let the soldier enter.

[*Exit* SERVANT]

[*Enter*] BOBADILL [*and*] MATTHEW

Now, sir, what ha' you to say to me?
BOBADILL
By your worship's favour –
CLEMENT
Nay, keep out, sir, I know not your pretence, you send me   50
word, sir, you are a soldier: why, sir, you shall be answered
here, here be them have been amongst soldiers. Sir, your
pleasure.
BOBADILL
Faith, sir, so it is, this gentleman and myself have been most
uncivilly wronged, and beaten, by one Downright, a coarse   55
fellow about the town here, and for mine own part, I
protest, being a man in no sort given to this filthy humour
of quarrelling, he hath assaulted me in the way of my peace;
despoiled me of mine honour; disarmed me of my weapons;
and rudely laid me along in the open streets, when I not so   60
much as once offered to resist him.
CLEMENT
Oh, God's precious! Is this the soldier? Here, take my
armour off quickly, 'twill make him swoon, I fear: he is not
fit to look on't, that will put up a blow.
MATTHEW
An't please your worship, he was bound to the peace.   65
CLEMENT
Why, an' he were, sir, his hands were not bound, were
they?

---

46 *gorget* a piece of armour for the throat (OED)
47 s.d. *Enter* BOBADILL *and* MATTHEW V.ii begins here in F.
50 *pretence* i.e. claim to my attention. This term may mean (as at III.iv.85) an asser-
   tion of a ground for legal action, and hence, business with Clement. But perhaps
   Clement, already observing Bobadill's cringing manner, is asking, 'Why are you
   pretending to be so meek?', or otherwise making fun of Bobadill's 'pretence' to
   be a soldier by asking, 'Why are you butting in?', assuming or pretending to
   assume this timid figure could not possibly be the anticipated soldier. Jackson
   specifies that Clement addresses this line to Matthew, but it is not necessarily so.
60 *laid me along* literally, stretched me at full length: laid me low
64 *put up* i.e. put up with, suffer quietly, patiently or tamely (OED put *v.*[1] 56.p.(a))

[*Enter* SERVANT]

SERVANT
There's one of the varlets of the City, sir, has brought two
gentlemen here, one upon your worship's warrant.
CLEMENT
My warrant?   70
SERVANT
Yes, sir. The officer says, procured by these two.
CLEMENT
Bid him come in. Set by this picture.

[*Exit* SERVANT]

[*Enter*] DOWNRIGHT, STEPHEN [*and*] BRAINWORM [*still*
disguised as a City sergeant]

What, Master Downright! Are you brought at Master
Freshwater's suit, here?
DOWNRIGHT
Aye, faith, sir. And here's another brought at my suit.   75
CLEMENT
What are you, sir?
STEPHEN
A gentleman, sir. Oh, uncle!
CLEMENT
Uncle? Who? Master Knowell?
KNOWELL
Aye, sir! This is a wise kinsman of mine.
STEPHEN
God's my witness, uncle, I am wronged here monstrously,   80
he charges me with stealing of his cloak, and would I might
never stir if I did not find it in the street, by chance.
DOWNRIGHT
Oh, did you find it, now? You said you bought it, erewhile.

---

72 *Set by this picture* i.e. Put aside, for the moment, this Bobadill, who is the mere
superficial likeness of a soldier, not a real one
73–4 *Master Freshwater's* Clement implies that the professed soldier Bobadill has
never seen battle, as a 'freshwater sailor' has never been to sea.
75 *Aye, faith* V.iii begins here in F; this might instead be read 'I'faith', but since it
is set up with a block 'I' to begin the scene, I have felt free to differentiate it from
the instances discussed in the note to III.i.87 above.
suit In picking up on Clement's term, Downright is playing on the fact that
Stephen was arrested for wearing Downright's clothing.
81–2 *would I might never stir* i.e. cross my heart and hope to die; cf. Tilley S861
83 *erewhile* a little while ago

STEPHEN

And you said I stole it; nay, now my uncle is here, I'll do
well enough with you.   85

CLEMENT

Well, let this breathe a while; you, that have cause to com-
plain there, stand forth: had you my warrant for this gentleman's apprehension?

BOBADILL

Aye, an't please your worship.

CLEMENT

Nay, do not speak in passion so; where had you it?   90

BOBADILL

Of your clerk, sir.

CLEMENT

That's well! An' my clerk can make warrants, and my hand
not at 'em! Where is the warrant? Officer, have you it?

BRAINWORM

No, sir, your worship's man, Master Formal, bid me do it
for these gentlemen, and he would be my discharge.   95

CLEMENT

Why, Master Downright, are you such a novice, to be
served, and never see the warrant?

DOWNRIGHT

Sir. He did not serve it on me.

CLEMENT

No? How then?

DOWNRIGHT

Marry, sir, he came to me, and said, he must serve it, and   100
he would use me kindly, and so –

CLEMENT

Oh, God's pity, was it so, sir? He must serve it? Give me my
long-sword there, and help me off; so. Come on, sir varlet,
I must cut off your legs, sirrah.

Flourishes over [the kneeling BRAINWORM] *with his*
long-sword

Nay, stand up, I'll use you kindly; I must cut off your legs,   105
I say.

---

86 *breathe* rest

90 *in passion so* i.e. with such strong feeling (spoken ironically; Clement continues
     to mock Bobadill's claim to be a fearsome soldier)

92–3 *my hand not at 'em* without my signing them

95 *be my discharge* i.e. take the responsibility, protect me from liability

103 *off* take off my robe

BRAINWORM
Oh, good sir, I beseech you; nay, good Master Justice.
CLEMENT
I must do it: there is no remedy. I must cut off your legs,
sirrah, I must cut off your ears, you rascal, I must do it; I
must cut off your nose, I must cut off your head.   110
BRAINWORM
Oh, good your worship.
CLEMENT
Well, rise, how dost thou do, now? Dost thou feel thyself
well? Hast thou no harm?
BRAINWORM
No, I thank your good worship, sir.
CLEMENT
Why, so! I said, I must cut off thy legs, and I must cut off   115
thy arms, and I must cut off thy head; but I did not do it.
So, you said, you must serve this gentleman with my war-
rant, but you did not serve him. You knave, you slave, you
rogue, do you say you must? Sirrah, away with him, to the
jail, I'll teach you a trick, for your *must*, sir.   120
BRAINWORM
Good sir, I beseech you, be good to me.
CLEMENT
Tell him he shall to the jail, away with him, I say.
BRAINWORM
Nay, sir, if you will commit me, it shall be for committing
more than this: I will not lose, by my travail, any grain of
my fame certain. [*Pulls off his disguise*]   125
CLEMENT
How is this!
KNOWELL
My man, Brainworm!
STEPHEN
Oh yes, uncle. Brainworm has been with my cousin Edward
and I all this day.
CLEMENT
I told you all there was some device!   130
BRAINWORM
Nay, excellent Justice, since I have laid myself thus open to

124–5 *I will ... fame certain* i.e. I'm unwilling to keep working (at my disguise and
    plot) if (instead of keeping me out of jail) it is only going to deprive me of credit
    for my impressive performances; or, I will not lose – I swear by all my hard
    labour – any portion of my inevitable fame (by keeping my tricks secret)

you, now stand strong for me: both with your sword, and
your balance.

CLEMENT

Body o' me, a merry knave! Give me a bowl of sack. If he
belong to you, Master Knowell, I bespeak your patience.   135

BRAINWORM

That is it I have most need of. [*To* KNOWELL] Sir, if you'll
pardon me only, I'll glory in all the rest of my exploits.

KNOWELL

Sir, you know I love not to have my favours come hard
from me. You have your pardon; though I suspect you
shrewdly for being of counsel with my son, against me.   140

BRAINWORM

Yes, faith, I have, sir; though you retained me doubly this
morning for yourself: first, as Brainworm; after, as
Fitzsword. I was your reformed soldier, sir. 'Twas I sent
you to Cob's, upon the errand without end.

KNOWELL

Is it possible! Or that thou should'st disguise thy language 145
so, as I should not know thee?

BRAINWORM

Oh, sir, this has been the day of my metamorphosis! It is
not that shape alone that I have run through, today. I
brought this gentleman, Master Kitely, a message too, in
the form of Master Justice's man, here, to draw him out o'   150
the way, as well as your worship; while Master Wellbred
might make a conveyance of Mistress Bridget to my young
master.

KITELY

How! My sister stol'n away?

KNOWELL

My son is not married, I hope!   155

132–3 *your sword ... balance* i.e. your punitive power and your fairness. Justice was
   often represented in art as a goddess holding balanced scales, a sword, or both
   (OED *sb.* 7).
140 *shrewdly* strongly, acutely
   of counsel in conspiracy
141 *retained* engaged by the payment of a preliminary fee, in order to secure services
   for one's own cause if necessary (OED). Since the word applied particularly to
   barristers, Brainworm is playing on the legal sense of 'counsel'.
143 *reformed* See III.iii.15n.
144 *errand without end* pointless trip; colloquially, wild goose chase
152 *conveyance* the transference of property ... from one person to another by any
   lawful act (OED); Brainworm continues the legal parlance of line 141.

BRAINWORM

Faith, sir, they are both as sure as love, a priest, and three
thousand pound (which is her portion) can make 'em; and
by this time are ready to bespeak their wedding supper at
the Windmill, except some friend, here, prevent 'em, and
invite 'em home.   160

CLEMENT

Marry, that will I (I thank thee for putting me in mind
on't). Sirrah, go you, and fetch 'em hither, upon my warrant.

[*Exit* SERVANT]

Neither's friends have cause to be sorry, if I know the
young couple aright. Here, I drink to thee, for thy good 165
news. But, I pray thee, what hast thou done with my man
Formal?

BRAINWORM

Faith, sir, after some ceremony past, as making him drunk,
first with story, and then with wine (but all in kindness) and
stripping him to his shirt, I left him in that cool vein, 170
departed, sold your worship's warrant to these two,
pawned his livery for that varlet's gown, to serve it in; and
thus have brought myself, by my activity, to your worship's
consideration.

CLEMENT

And I will consider thee in another cup of sack. Here's to 175
thee, which having drunk off, this is my sentence. Pledge
me. Thou hast done or assisted to nothing, in my judgement, but deserves to be pardoned for the wit o' the
offence. If thy master, or any man here, be angry with thee,
I shall suspect his ingine, while I know him, for't. How 180
now? What noise is that?

[*Enter* SERVANT]

SERVANT

Sir, it is Roger is come home.

---

156 *sure* joined in wedlock (OED)

159 *prevent* forestall

170 *stripping him to his shirt* i.e. taking off all his outer clothing (waistcoat, doublet,
  etc.)

  vein fashion; temporary state of mind or feeling (OED); possibly also, flow of
  liquid

176–7 *Pledge me* i.e. Drink with me

180 *I ... for't* i.e. I shall doubt his intellect, for as long as I know him, on that
  account

CLEMENT
Bring him in, bring him in.

[*Enter*] FORMAL [*in a suit of armour*]

What! Drunk in arms, against me? Your reason, your
reason for this?   185

FORMAL
I beseech your worship to pardon me: I happened into ill
company by chance, that cast me into a sleep, and stripped
me of all my clothes –

CLEMENT
Well, tell him I am Justice Clement, and do pardon him;
but, what is this to your armour? What may that signify?   190

FORMAL
An't please you, sir, it hung up i' the room where I was
stripped; and I borrowed it of one o' the drawers, to come
home in, because I was loath to do penance through the
street i' my shirt.

CLEMENT
Well, stand by a while. Who be these?   195

[*Enter*] EDWARD, WELLBRED, [*and*] BRIDGET

Oh, the young company, welcome, welcome. Gi' you joy.
Nay, Mistress Bridget, blush not: you are not so fresh a
bride but the news of it is come hither afore you. Master
bridegroom, I ha' made your peace, give me your hand; so
will I for all the rest, ere you forsake my roof.   200

EDWARD
We are the more bound to your humanity, sir.

---

184 *in arms* Rushing into court wielding weapons was presumably even more offen-
     sive if the bearer of the arms was drunk; Clement's joke is that Formal is 'in
     arms' only in a narrow, literal sense. The stripped man returning to town wear-
     ing armour was a familiar comic motif.
186 *I beseech* V.iv begins here in F (because of Formal's entrance in the preceding
     lines).
190 *what ... armour?* i.e. what does this have to do with your armour?
192 *drawers* tapsters, bartenders
193–4 *do penance ... shirt* Walking the streets wearing only a white sheet (a shirt
     was sometimes permitted underneath) was a form of shaming punishment often
     imposed for moral offences.
201 *We are the more* V.v begins here in F (because of the entrances in the preceding
     lines).
     bound indebted

CLEMENT
  Only these two have so little of man in 'em, they are no part
  of my care.
WELLBRED
  Yes, sir, let me pray you for this gentleman, [*Indicating*
  MATTHEW] he belongs to my sister, the bride.   205
CLEMENT
  In what place, sir?
WELLBRED
  Of her delight, sir, below the stairs, and in public: her poet,
  sir.
CLEMENT
  A poet? I will challenge him myself, presently, at *extem-*
  pore: 210
  '*Mount up thy Phlegon muse, and testify,*
  How Saturn, sitting in an ebon cloud,
  Disrobed his podex white as ivory,
  And, through the welkin, thund'red all aloud.'
WELLBRED
  He is not for *extempore*, sir. He is all for the pocket-muse, 215
  please you command a sight of it.
CLEMENT
  Yes, yes, search him for a taste of his vein.

206 *place* employment, position, or capacity
207 *Of her delight* i.e. As the person assigned to please her, or, In whatever place
    pleases her, with a sexual *double entendre* in either case
    below the stairs i.e. in the role of a servant, or in the lower quarters (picking up
    earlier bawdy analogies between Bridget's body and a house); the *double enten-*
    dre of the previous phrase is now quadruple.
211 *Mount up thy Phlegon muse* i.e. Get on the fiery horse that is your muse (per-
    haps addressed to Matthew); or, Get on your fiery horse, muse (H&S identifies
    Phlegon as one of the horses of the Sun); cf. Shakespeare's call for a 'Muse of
    fire' in the choral opening line of *Henry V.*
212 *Saturn* a powerful Roman god, associated with the Greek Chronos (time) and
    hence old age, but also (Jackson points out) associated in this period with fart-
    ing and defecation
    ebon black
213 *podex* rump; '*Saturni podex* was proverbial for anything or anyone decrepit,
    worn out, or senseless' (Jackson, noting H&S, cites Erasmus, *Adagia*, ed.
    Stephanus, 1558, col. 808).
214 *welkin* sky
    thund'red farted
217 *taste of his vein* i.e. sample of his style; 'taste one's vein' also meant 'feel one's
    pulse', so may suggest grabbing Matthew by the wrist.

[They search the pockets of MATTHEW, *who resists]*

WELLBRED

You must not deny the Queen's Justice, sir, under a writ o'
rebellion.

CLEMENT

What! All this verse? Body o' me, he carries a whole realm,   220
a commonwealth of paper, in's hose! Let's see some of his
subjects! *[Reads]*
'*Unto the boundless Ocean of thy face,*
Runs this poor river charged with streams of eyes.'
How? This is stol'n!   225

EDWARD

A parody! A parody! With a kind of miraculous gift to
make it absurder than it was.

CLEMENT

Is all the rest, of this batch? Bring me a torch: lay it
together, and give fire. Cleanse the air. Here was enough to
have infected the whole City, if it had not been taken in   230
time.

[The papers are burned]

See, see, how our poet's glory shines! Brighter and brighter!
Still it increases! Oh, now it's at the highest; and now it
declines as fast. You may see. *Sic transit gloria mundi.*

KNOWELL

There's an emblem for you, son, and your studies!   235

218–19 *deny ... rebellion* i.e. resist (a search by) royally-appointed authorities, sir,
  or you will be liable for an arrest-warrant for 'disobedience to a legal summons'
  (OED rebellion¹ 1.c)

220 *realm* a variant spelling of 'ream'; this pun was popular in the sixteenth century,
  before the spellings 'realm' for 'a kingdom' and 'ream' for 'a quantity of paper'
  became standard.

222 *subjects* i.e. topics of his verse, with a pun on the 'subjects' or citizens of the
  'commonwealth of paper' that inhabits Matthew's stockings

223–4 These lines burlesque the first lines of Daniel's sonnet sequence *Delia* (1592):
  'Unto the boundless ocean of thy beauty / Runs this poor river, charged with
  streams of zeal'.

228 *batch* the sort of 'lot' to which a thing belongs by origin (as loaves do to their
  own batch) (OED); see I.i.164–5

228–9 Clement here performs a mock version of actual measures commonly taken
  against the plague.

234 *Sic ... mundi* 'So [quickly] passes away the glory of this world', a common
  proverb in both languages

235 *emblem* picture expressing a moral fable (OED)

CLEMENT

Nay, no speech or act of mine be drawn against such as
profess it worthily. They are not born every year, as an
alderman. There goes more to the making of a good poet,
than a sheriff, Master Kitely. You look upon me! Though I
live i' the City here, amongst you, I will do more reverence 240
to him, when I meet him, than I will to the mayor, out of
his year. But, these paper-pedlars! These ink-dabblers!
They cannot expect reprehension, or reproach. They have it
with the fact.

EDWARD

Sir, you have saved me the labour of a defence.   245

CLEMENT

It shall be discourse for supper: between your father and
me, if he dare undertake me. But, to dispatch away these,
you sign o' the Soldier, and picture o' the Poet (but both so
false I will not ha' you hanged out at my door till midnight), while we are at supper, you two shall penitently fast 250
it out in my court, without; and, if you will, you may pray
there, that we may be so merry within as to forgive, or
forget you, when we come out. Here's a third, because we

236–7 *Nay ... worthily* i.e. No, let nothing I say or do be construed or adduced to
    discredit good poets
237–8 *They ... alderman* Adapted from a passage Jonson's *Discoveries* misattributes
    to Petronius: '*Consules fiunt quotannis ... solus aut rex aut poeta non quotan-
    nis nascitur*' ('Consuls are made annually ... only a king or poet is not born
    every year'); Florus, *De Qualitate Vitae*, cited by H&S.
241–2 *out ... year* i.e. when his one-year term is over
243–4 *They cannot ... fact* This probably means, 'They cannot, or don't have to,
    wait for criticism: the work disgraces itself', though the easiest sense is offered
    by emending 'expect' to 'escape'.
245 *saved me ... defence* Instead of this exchange, the Quarto version gives the
    Edward character (there named Lorenzo) a thirty-two line speech in defence of
    poetry. Critics generally attribute this cut to Jonson's maturation as a play-
    wright, but – along with other cuts in this final scene – it could conceivably
    reflect instead the Folio printer's determination to compress the text into the
    space he had left for it.
248–50 *sign ... midnight* As when he called Bobadill 'this picture' at l. 72 above,
    Clement suggests here that both men are frauds, like misleading shop or inn signs
    – or at least ones so embarrassing that he would hang them in front of his house
    only when no one would see them.
250–1 *penitently fast it out in my court, without* i.e. repent by going hungry in my
    courtyard, outside
253 *a third* i.e. Formal, still in armour

tender your safety, shall watch you, he is provided for the
purpose. [*To* FORMAL] Look to your charge, sir.   255
STEPHEN
   And what shall I do?
CLEMENT
   Oh, I had lost a sheep, an' he had not bleated! Why, sir, you
   shall give Master Downright his cloak; and I will entreat
   him to take it. A trencher and a napkin you shall have, i'
   the buttery, and keep Cob and his wife company, here;   260
   whom I will entreat first to be reconciled, and you to
   endeavour with your wit to keep 'em so.
STEPHEN
   I'll do my best.
COB
   Why, now I see thou art honest, Tib, I receive thee as my
   dear and mortal wife again.   265
TIB
   And I you, as my loving and obedient husband.
CLEMENT
   Good complement! It will be their bridal night too. They
   are married anew. Come, I conjure the rest to put off all
   discontent. You, Master Downright, your anger; you,
   Master Knowell, your cares; Master Kitely, and his wife,   270
   their jealousy.
   For, I must tell you both, while that is fed,
   Horns i' the mind are worse than o' the head.
KITELY
   Sir, thus they go from me; kiss me, sweetheart.
   '*See what a drove of horns fly in the air,*   275
   Winged with my cleansèd, and my credulous breath!
   Watch 'em, suspicious eyes, watch where they fall.
   See, see! On heads, that think they've none at all!
   Oh, what a plenteous world of this will come!

254 *tender* care for, value (OED)
259–60 *A trencher ... buttery* i.e. You will eat with the servants in the pantry
265 *mortal* deadly (Cob's mistake for 'moral')
266 *obedient* Tib here reverses the marriage service, in which it is the wife who vows
    to obey.
267 *complement* (1) completion, consummation; (2) ceremoniousness; formal civil-
    ity, politeness, or courtesy (OED); (3) reciprocity (of errors in these renewed
    vows)
272 *while that is fed* i.e. while the humour of jealousy is being fed. Versions of this
    couplet were commonplace in the period.
275 *drove* a driven herd

When air rains horns, all may be sure of some.'   280
I ha' learned so much verse out of a jealous man's part in a
play.
CLEMENT
'Tis well, 'tis well! This night we'll dedicate to friendship,
love, and laughter. Master bridegroom, take your bride,
and lead; every one, a fellow. Here is my mistress: 285
Brainworm! To whom all my addresses of courtship shall
have their reference. Whose adventures this day, when our
grandchildren shall hear to be made a fable, I doubt not but
it shall find both spectators, and applause.

[*Exeunt*]

280 *some* F replaces 'some' with 'fame', which conceivably suits the reasoning of the
passage, but surely breaks its rhyme; I therefore join the other modern editors in
emending to the reading from Q and F2, especially since the old-style 's' could
have made the words look much alike to the F type-setter.
281–2 *I ... play* No such play has been identified.
285 *every one, a fellow* i.e. each with a partner
286–7 *To ... reference* i.e. To whom I will direct all my courtship; an extension of
Brainworm's role as Clement's chosen 'mistress' for this wedding celebration,
and probably a play on the two chief meanings of 'court'.
287–9 *Whose ... applause* An invitation, often found at the end of Renaissance
plays, for the audience to begin applauding.

Printed in the USA
CPSIA information can be obtained
at www.ICGtesting.com
LVHW020839171024
794056LV00002B/292